Integratin~

Integrating CBT and Third Wave Therapies offers a thought-through approach to integrating evidence-based therapies. It provides help for all of us who are developing or have expertise in a variety of evidence-based approaches.

The theoretical part of the book briefly reviews four therapies, namely: CBT, DBT, ACT and CFT. The authors identify core processes of change and examine how each therapy contributes to each core process, helping in the integration of all four. The text considers the influence of early adversity on later mental wellbeing, the theoretical underpinnings of mindfulness, behaviour analysis, re-living and re-scripting and dissociation. Theory and practice chapters are illustrated using case vignettes.

The book will be useful for therapists to structure sessions with clients. It demonstrates how to follow a theoretical approach and offers a therapeutic structure for integrated clinical work. It will be useful in reflective practice and supervision, and for students learning about a variety of therapeutic approaches.

Fiona Kennedy is an award-winning clinician, researcher, trainer and author. She is a Director of GreenWood Mentors, providing therapy, supervision and training. She specialises in trauma and its consequences, especially dissociation, and in integrating CBT and third wave therapies. She volunteers in India each year, helping NGOs to provide and research into nurturing care for young people in adversity.

David Pearson's career has been with the UK National Health Service as a Consultant Clinical Psychologist. Currently, he is a Director of GreenWood Mentors, an Advisor for the NGO, Dream a Dream, and an award-winning author. Designing interventions and assessments following severe childhood adversity and integrating therapy to meet the needs of individuals have been life-long interests.

CBT Distinctive Features

Series Editor: Windy Dryden

Cognitive behaviour therapy (CBT) occupies a central position in the move towards evidence-based practice and is frequently used in the clinical environment. Yet there is no one universal approach to CBT and clinicians speak of first, second and even third wave approaches.

This series provides straightforward, accessible guides to a number of CBT methods, clarifying the distinctive features of each approach. The series editor, Windy Dryden, successfully brings together experts from each discipline to summarise the 30 main aspects of their approach divided into theoretical and practical features.

The CBT Distinctive Features Series will be essential reading for psychotherapists, counsellors and psychologists of all orientations who want to learn more about the range of new and developing cognitive behaviour approaches.

Recent titles in the series:

For further information about this series please visit
www.routledge.com/CBT-Distinctive-Features/book-series/DFS

Integrating CBT and Third Wave Therapies

Distinctive Features

Fiona Kennedy
and David Pearson

Routledge
Taylor & Francis Group

LONDON AND NEW YORK

First published 2021
by Routledge
2 Park Square, Milton Park, Abingdon, Oxon OX14 4RN

and by Routledge
52 Vanderbilt Avenue, New York, NY 10017

Routledge is an imprint of the Taylor & Francis Group, an informa business

British Library Cataloguing-in-Publication Data
A catalogue record for this book is available from the British Library

Library of Congress Cataloging-in-Publication Data
A catalog record has been requested for this book

ISBN: 978-1-138-33666-7 (hbk)
ISBN: 978-1-138-33667-4 (pbk)
ISBN: 978-0-429-44292-6 (ebk)

Typeset in Times New Roman
Swales & Willis, Exeter, Devon, UK

Contents

Introduction

This book is for therapists and other people in helping roles. It is designed to stand alone or to be used alongside our book *Get Your Life Back: The Most Effective Therapies for a Better You*, which is written for clients (and therapists) to use directly as a work book. This current book addresses how to integrate four of the most popular evidence-based therapies in use at the moment: CBT (cognitive behaviour therapy) and three 'third wave' therapies: DBT (dialectical behaviour therapy), ACT (acceptance and commitment therapy) and CFT (compassion focused therapy). Each of these therapies has developed and expanded to include applications to a wide variety of client presentations and has incorporated mindfulness and acceptance focused interventions. Each has borrowed and includes interventions and concepts from the others. Although there is a lively debate about similarities and differences between the approaches, particularly as to the role and importance of cognitions and the processes of change, they have many theoretical and practical aspects in common.

In the first part of this book, the basic theory of each approach is outlined 'in a nutshell'. Theoretical similarities and differences are examined, as are ways to resolve or tolerate apparent conflicts between theories. Fundamental theoretical principles and core processes of change are discussed. We see these as key to a new therapy, CBT+, which integrates the four approaches. The second part of the book uses clinical vignettes as practical illustrations. It offers basic therapeutic principles and a protocol for CBT+. NAVIGATES is an acronym for how to proceed with CBT+ in a way that makes sense to therapists and clients.

In Part I, Chapters 2 to 5 briefly describe in a nutshell CBT, DBT, ACT and CFT, with emphasis on the theory underpinning the practice of each therapy. A discussion of some reasons for and against integrating the approaches follows in Chapter 6. For example, it is undoubtedly the case that most clinicians are attending trainings in some or all of these therapies. We are then returning to our own practice and using the ideas and techniques we have learned. But do we have the opportunity to think through why and how we are choosing what to use from moment to moment? Another consideration is that integration is already happening, for example with the establishment of mindfulness-based CBT. DBT and ACT each borrow heavily from other approaches, including CFT. Having summarised the basic theory and practice of each therapeutic approach and discussed pros and cons of integration, we look at commonalities and differences between CBT, DBT, ACT and CFT. We argue that a dialectical stance is needed where apparent opposites can be held in mind simultaneously. When we think about how to describe light, we need to think about both waves and particles to fully account for its behaviour; when we think about human beings, we need to hold apparently contradictory concepts in mind to fully account for our behaviour. A contextualist approach, where everything can be understood only within its context, forms the basic philosophical platform on which to build an integrated therapy.

Chapter 7 expands on the behavioural underpinnings of CBT+. By looking at what we know about processes of change in therapy, Chapters 8 and 9 show how we can aim to guide clients through core processes of change.

The acronym NAVIGATES is introduced in Chapter 10, as a memory aid or protocol to describe what needs to happen in CBT+ therapy to turn all this theory into practice.

In Chapter 11 we take some time to understand why childhood trauma of various kinds is so important in the development of later mental health problems. In Chapter 12 we look at the theoretical underpinnings of mindfulness, and in Chapter 13 behavioural theory. Chapter 14 explores some of the theory involved in re-living and re-scripting approaches for trauma, and Chapter 15 presents some theory to help us understand dissociative responding, especially after trauma.

In Part II, the acronym NAVIGATES is looked at in more detail. Chapters 16 and 17 introduce two complex cases, Ruth and Stuart, which will be used as illustrations of CBT+ work. Teaching mindfulness to clients is the topic of Chapter 18, as it is an essential therapist stance in CBT+ and central to skills taught to clients. Chapter 19 contains useful practical mindfulness exercises. Chapter 20 shows how to get commitment and motivation from both client and the therapist. This happens before the therapy itself, using a DBT 'pre-therapy' approach: problems of motivation and commitment are among the blocks to change in 'challenging' presentations. Chapters 21 to 29 are based around the mnemonic NAVIGATES. Each letter prompts the therapist to do certain things, but with a considerable amount of discretion as to how to achieve the aim and in which order to take each step. NAVIGATES allows the therapist to guide the client through the core processes of change. The core processes of change involve: developing the ability to take new perspectives on one's experiences and behaviour; having or acquiring the motivation and skills to act differently to one's established habits in response to distressing emotions; reprocessing trauma, childhood abuse and neglect; and becoming willing and able to relate to oneself and others with compassion and trust.

The summary and conclusions in Chapter 30 emphasise that CBT+ is a principle-driven approach. It is not prescriptive but focused on guiding the client through the processes needed to produce therapeutic change. It seems essential that we draw on all the currently available knowledge and skills in order to do this.

Part I

THE DISTINCTIVE THEORETICAL FEATURES OF CBT+

CBT in a nutshell

What is CBT?

Cognitive behavioural therapy (CBT) was one of the most important advances in therapy of the 20th century. As the name suggests, CBT developed in the 1950s and 1960s with the combination of cognitive therapy and behaviour therapy. This advance is generally attributed to Aaron T. Beck (Thomas, Pilecki & McKay, 2015).

How CBT conceptualises psychological distress

The way we think about things affects how we feel, what we do and our bodily responses. Let us take the example of Rengina. She believes she will not be able to get on the bus, because she predicts people will look at her and think bad things about her. She avoids bus stops as she feels a great deal of anxiety. She is afraid people will notice her panic and believes that her symptoms mean she might have a heart attack. She notices that when she walks away from the bus stop the horrible sickly, sweaty feelings disappear. These thoughts and feelings are the driving force for her avoidance of bus stops. Most mental health problems are driven by avoidance and anxiety. Rengina can prevent some feelings of anxiety by avoiding leaving the house so that she does not see a bus or bus stop. Of course, there are big costs of this avoidance behaviour.

If Rengina saw a therapist she might say that she is afraid of leaving the house. Leaving the house gives her sensations of panic. She feels sick, her body shakes and she has thoughts that she will have a heart attack. These are experiences that everybody would want to avoid, but interestingly not leaving the house has the advantage of reducing those awful feelings and thoughts at the bus stop. A CBT formulation would identify the components of Rengina's experience. Beck described these components as 'schemas', a concept introduced by Piaget (Beck, 1967). A schema is an underlying neurological structure, formed by our previous learning or by being hardwired from birth. It determines how we interpret and respond to our environment. There are four types of schemas:

> *Thoughts* ('I don't want to leave the house in case I see a bus'; 'I am too unwell to go out'; 'People look at me and think I am inferior')
> *Feelings* (fear, shame)
> *Body sensations* (nausea, fast heartbeat, shaking, breathing fast and shallow)
> *Behaviour* (stay at home, decide not to go out)

The CBT formulation is commonly known as a 'Hot-cross-Bun' or 'Wheel of Experience' and looks like the diagram in Figure 2.1.

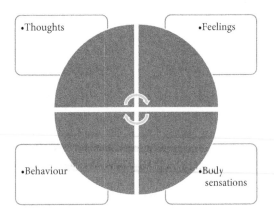

Figure 2.1 Hot-cross Bun or Wheel of Experience CBT formulation

There is a fifth element to this formulation, which is the environment or context in which the schemas are activated. In Rengina's case, this could be when she needs to go out and get shopping, meet friends, etc. Then she will start thinking about what might happen if she goes out, or else she might even just experience anxiety and all the symptoms without consciously thinking about going out. This 'five areas model' is explained by Williams and colleagues (e.g., Williams, 2001; Wright, Williams & Garland, 2002). The environmental triggers for responses can be internal events, such as thoughts, images, memories or body sensations (for example, Rengina thinking 'I'm out of butter, I'll need to go out to the shop'). They can also be external events, such as seeing a program on TV, something someone says, or the arrival of a bus at the bus stop. Certain situations may also act as 'setting conditions' or signals for these responses (for Rengina, the bus stop or a group of people).

A central tenet of CBT is that it is *not events or situations themselves that cause distress, but the interpretation of them*. This is often illustrated using the example of the 'noise in the night'. Being woken by a crashing noise, one could think 'Oh, it's the cat'. In this case we might feel a little annoyed. Or we could interpret the *same* noise as being a burglar downstairs, in which case terror might be our response. Our internal schemas determine our interpretations and responses.

Negative thoughts can happen often and are 'automatic' and unquestioned by the person having them. The CBT shorthand for this is NATs (negative automatic thoughts).

Personality can be formulated as a 'deep structure' of 'core beliefs' about the self, the world and other people. These beliefs are likely to have been formed early in life and be hard to change. They lead to 'underlying assumptions' about the way things are, which in turn produce NATs.

For Rengina:

NAT:	'People will stare at me on the bus'
Underlying assumption:	'If people notice me they will think I'm weird'
Core belief:	(self) 'I'm defective' – (others) 'are judgemental' – (world) 'is dangerous and cruel'

How does CBT help us to change?

CBT aims to change thoughts that are driving behaviours. It may also be appropriate to directly change behaviours that will in turn change thoughts. The key processes are as follows:

- The client records and reviews their thoughts with help from the therapist
- The client is helped to notice that their thoughts link to their feelings, behaviour and bodily responses
- The therapist focuses on identifying emotion-laden 'hot' thoughts, using a CBT formulation
- Jointly with the client, the therapist explores the problem with curiosity, using 'Socratic' questions about the client's thoughts and feelings, for example 'How do you know that?' or 'Where did you learn that?'

CBT teaches thought handling skills. Below are some of these skills with examples:

- Perspective taking: 'What would someone who disagrees with you say?'; 'Just helicopter up and look down at the situation … then decide what you want to do'
- Compassion: 'What would a kind friend say about that?'; 'What would you say to your own loved one if they told you this?'
- Mindfulness: 'Can we just observe and describe this thought or feeling, without trying to change it and without getting caught up in it?'

CBT can also work to directly to change behaviour, especially when the client is stuck in avoidant inactivity:
    'Let's get active when you feel low, don't wait until you feel like it, perhaps using activity scheduling'

The effectiveness of CBT

This necessarily basic account of CBT does not include the vast array of adaptations of the therapy to different problems. There is an impressive amount of convincing evidence for the effectiveness of CBT (Hofmann et al., 2012; Thomas, Pilecki & McKay, 2015).

CBT has led the way in conducting randomised controlled trials comparing treatments with medication. It has also aligned itself with the psychiatric classifications found in manuals such as ICD-10 and DSM V, leading to increased understanding and acceptance in the medical world. The English IAPT (Improving Access to Psychological Therapies) service is leading the way globally in providing CBT for specific conditions, producing a vast database of outcomes (Hofmann et al., 2012).

Summary

CBT is:

- A joint effort, with client collaboration
- Focused on emotional and behavioural change, often through working with negative automatic thoughts
- Backed by very considerable evidence that it is effective

References

American Psychiatric Association. (2013). *Diagnostic and Statistical Manual of Mental Disorders*, 5th Edition. Washington, DC: APA.

Beck, A. T. (1967). *Depression: Clinical, Experimental, and Theoretical Aspects*. New York: Harper & Row. (Republished as *Depression: Causes and Treatment*. Philadelphia: University of Pennsylvania Press. 1972).

Hofmann, S. G., Asnaani, A., Vonk, I. J., Sawyer, A. T., & Fang, A. (2012). The efficacy of cognitive behavioral therapy: A review of meta-analyses. *Cognitive Therapy and Research*, *36*(5), 427–440.

Thomas, N., Pilecki, B., & McKay, D. (2015). A review of theory, history, and evidence. *Psychodynamic Psychiatry*, *43*(3), 423–461.

Williams, C. J. (2001). *Overcoming Depression: A Five Areas Approach*. London: Arnold.

World Health Organization. (2016). *The ICD-10 Classification of Mental and Behavioural Disorders*. Geneva: WHO.

Wright, B., Williams, C., & Garland, A. (2002). Using the five areas cognitive–behavioural therapy model with psychiatric patients. *Advances in Psychiatric Treatment*, *8*(4), 307–315.

3

ACT in a nutshell

What is ACT?

Acceptance and commitment therapy (ACT) uses mindfulness, acceptance and a focus on committed, values-based action to help people make changes in their lives. Its development is generally ascribed to Steven Hayes and colleagues (Hayes, Strosahl & Wilson, 2016).

ACT does not focus on symptom reduction per se, although symptoms often do change during an ACT intervention. Rather, it focuses on increasing 'psychological flexibility': the ability to stay focused on and moving towards the things that give meaning and purpose to our lives, our values.

Acceptance is needed because uncomfortable, unwanted thoughts and feelings are an inevitable part of life. A life that is fully lived, rich, fun and fulfilling *must* involve willingly exposing oneself to unpleasant experiences. Human beings are 'hard-wired' to avoid unpleasant internal and external stimuli. So making progress, using ACT, requires the client to understand the reasons *why* they need to feel unpleasant things, become *willing* to feel unpleasant things and get *skilled* in doing so. For example, I might have a personal goal to climb a mountain because I value achievement and adventure. But I am likely to experience exhaustion, discomfort and possibly despair on the way up the mountain. It is part of the package. In accepting this and learning how to deal with it without giving up, I will greatly improve my chances of success in following my values.

How ACT conceptualises psychological distress

Much human suffering comes from emotional avoidance: instinct-driven behaviour that helps us to avoid or escape from pain. Avoidance responses are strengthened each time they occur as they lead to *relief*, which is a change of internal state from an aversive to a less aversive state. This process is known as 'negative reinforcement', meaning we will repeat and expand our avoidant responses. For example, Rengina, who is afraid people may look at her and judge her as she travels on the bus, experiences distress as she thinks about doing this. When she decides not to do that today, she experiences relief. The problem with this emotional avoidance strategy is that it produces short-term gain but long-term pain. Our lives eventually shrink to nothing at all interesting, as we consciously or unconsciously avoid or escape from unpleasant stimuli.

ACT's theory of language, relational frame theory (RFT), describes how humans give meaning to their experiences based on previous learning. Rengina has learned that travelling on the bus is a scary, threatening experience. But these meanings can become an invisible cage, which keeps us trapped in avoidant responding. Because Rengina never travels on the bus she does not have a chance to learn that she can manage her fear. Our human language skills allow us to form complex societies and to rule the world. However, we can also suffer as our thoughts take us time travelling, going backwards and forwards in time: ruminating on the past and worrying about the future.

Psychological flexibility is the opposite of emotional avoidance. It is a willingness to experience everything life brings and to act on our values. ACT proposes psychological flexibility as the key to a meaningful life.

The 'hexaflex' is a popular ACT formulation tool. It describes six core psychological processes needed for psychological flexibility, these are:

- Acceptance
- Defusion
- Present moment awareness
- Self as context
- Values
- Committed action

ACT therapists can assess their clients using the 'triflex': a simplified version of the hexaflex:

- Open
- Aware
- Active

The therapist, using the triflex, asks 'How open, aware and active is the client?' 'Open' means, can the client accept what is happening right now and have some distance from their own thoughts and feelings? 'Aware' means can the person stay focused in the present moment and take an observing self (rather than a thinking self) perspective on what is happening? 'Active' means is the person clear on what really matters to them in life, and are they taking action to move towards these things?

The answers for Rengina would be that she is not *open* to experiencing the distress that riding on the bus would cause her. Understandably, she is driven by her thoughts, mental images and feelings of threat. She is using avoidant coping strategies such as deciding not to take a bus journey, so that her *awareness* is narrowed to noticing only her fear. She is not *active* in pursuing her values, one of which involves attending college, which would require getting the bus.

Rengina's ACT formulation may look something like the image in Figure 3.1.

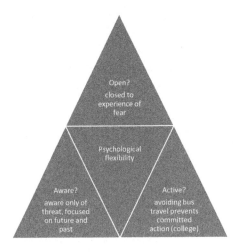

Figure 3.1 Rengina's ACT formulation

How does ACT help us to change?

At the same time as formulating a client's distress using 'open, aware and active', the ACT therapist will be working on the client's commitment to therapy. This may start with the use of 'creative hopelessness'. Here, the therapist will listen carefully, validating the client's distress and making sure all of the client's previous efforts to solve the problem or feel better have been heard. Then the therapist might ask 'So, all of these efforts you've made, despite trying as hard as you can, have not worked? Would you be willing to try something different?' We can see here the beginnings of working on willingness, another word for openness. Then the therapist may orientate the client to the ACT approach by explaining that as a team they will be working on changing the client's *relationship to* his or her thoughts and feelings, rather than on changing the thoughts and feelings themselves. The idea is to enable the client to function well, keeping moving towards a valued life, however they may feel from day to day.

ACT therapy includes getting clear on the client's values. The metaphor, 'my 80th birthday party', involves asking the client to imagine it is their 80th birthday and everyone they have ever admired or loved can be there. What would the client like to hear being said about them? Usually this work results in some descriptions of how the client would ideally like to be in various contexts, such as work, relationships, health and leisure. These might look like 'In my relationship with my son I want to be loving, supportive and available'.

From here we can progress to setting goals related to these values. For example, 'I want to spend some time just being with and focused on my son'. Smaller, specific and measurable goals should follow, for example, 'Tonight I'll be with my son from 6 to 7 pm and make sure I'm not interrupted by turning my phone off'. The client will have a chance to go home and try out this plan over the following week. We have described a desired behavioural change and agreed that the client will take committed action towards it.

Most people discover that obstacles come up, which get in the way of smooth progress towards these goals. These may be practical or external issues such as unexpected visitors arriving at 6 pm and having to be catered for. However, much of the time they are internal obstacles, involving thoughts, feelings, body sensations or problem behaviours. For example, Rengina states she values learning new things. Her goal is to attend college each day. But her fear and deciding not to get on the bus get in the way.

The therapist uses many ACT metaphors and role plays to facilitate experiential learning about how avoidance maintains problems and how acceptance and approach behaviours can change one's life. The client gains new skills in relating differently to internal events and taking action towards clear goals and values.

The effectiveness of ACT

ACT is backed by an extensive body of research demonstrating its effectiveness across a range of issues, including psychosis, depression, anxiety, substance misuse and addiction, anger and chronic pain (Hayes, Strosahl & Wilson, 2016).

Suggested further reading

Harris, R. (2006). *ACT Made Simple: An Easy-To-Read Primer on Acceptance and Commitment Therapy*. Oakland, CA: New Harbinger.

Oliver, J., Hill, J., & Morris, E. (2016). *ACTivate Your Life: Using Acceptance and Mindfulness to Build a Life that Is Rich, Fulfilling and Fun*. London: Little Brown.

Reference

Hayes, S. C., Strosahl, K. D., & Wilson, K. G. (2016). *Acceptance and Commitment Therapy: The Process and Practice of Mindful Change*, 2nd Edition. New York: Guilford Press.

4

DBT in a nutshell

What is DBT?

Dialectical behaviour therapy (DBT) was developed to help in particular with presentations that therapists find difficult to address. Initially Marsha Linehan (e.g., 2006) worked with people attempting suicide and with borderline personality disorder (BPD, also known as emotionally unstable personality disorder or EUPD). DBT is an approach based on behavioural analysis. It incorporates mindfulness and acceptance from Zen Buddhism, and holds these two seemingly opposite approaches together within a dialectical world view. Dialectics is a philosophical approach that holds that things are constantly in flux and changing, and that there is no 'Truth', only points of view or perspectives that depend on the context. Dialectics involves the concept that wherever there is a stated perspective (a thesis), there is also the opposite perspective (the antithesis). There will also be a third perspective that can incorporate the thesis and the antithesis (the synthesis). For example, I might argue that money is the root of all evil (thesis). You might say that money is a useful invention that makes trading and travel much easier and does a lot of good in the world (antithesis). We might both eventually agree that money in itself is neither good nor evil, but can be used for many purposes, including doing good or evil things (synthesis). Dialectics is important in DBT as an alternative to taking a judgemental stance and arguing with clients and others in the caring system.

How DBT conceptualises psychological distress

Problems with emotional regulation are seen as central to many problem presentations. This means being very sensitive (having a low threshold) to emotional triggers, becoming overly emotionally aroused and taking longer to calm down or restore equilibrium. Problem behaviours such as self-harm, attempting suicide, gambling, addictions, eating disorders and more are seen as learned behaviours that have a function to produce emotional regulation or emotional change. For example, Tom, a solicitor, gets very stressed when he perceives he is being criticised. He responds by feeling a strong urge to go online and play poker. He has such a problem with gambling that in the past he has lost his house, his wife and his children because of it. Now in a new relationship and working to get more access to his children, he still feels an overwhelming urge to gamble most days. And he actually does go online and play several times a week.

The bio-social theory of BPD lays out how DBT sees maladaptive patterns of behaviour emerge through a person's development and history. On the biology side, there may be genetic predispositions to having a sensitive nervous system that is easily aroused and takes longer to soothe. There may be environmental factors, even from the baby's time in the womb, which interact with biological factors. These could include domestic abuse of the mother causing hormonal changes in the blood supply or injury to the baby, etc. Once the child is born, the parents may be unable to react effectively to the child's needs. They could be highly anxious and sensitive parents. They may be neglectful, perhaps abusive parents. Or they may be perfectionistic, emotionally unresponsive parents. All of these examples mean an 'invalidating' environment for the child, which in turn affects the child's biological functioning. The learning history from this context is carried with the person to new environments. For example, a learned behaviour of hair-pulling may have been reinforced in the context of an invalidating childhood home, where the parents have only reacted to distress when this behaviour happened. Later, in an adult relationship, the person may find that they hair-pull when they are distressed. Their partner may find this weird and disturbing and the person may be embarrassed to discuss it, leading to relationship stress and more hair-pulling.

Tom may have been *born* with an emotionally 'thin skin', we do not know. But we know his father was a high achiever who stressed self-discipline and pointed out every flaw in Tom's performance. At eight, Tom discovered slot machines at the local arcade. He began stealing money from his parents for the machines. He felt free and in control when he was gambling, better feelings than he had at home. DBT is ideal for such 'addictive', repetitive damaging behaviours.

Rengina's mother was cautious, anxious and suffered from social anxiety. Rengina learned to perceive other people as critical and to cope by avoiding getting near to them. Growing up she only felt safe around her mother. Now mum has died, she feels alone and unprotected. An adaptation from DBT 'radically open DBT' (roDBT, e.g. Lynch, 2018) addresses 'over-controlled', avoidant coping.

How does DBT help us to change?

There is a pre-therapy phase of client engagement in DBT, where the client and therapist discuss whether or not to proceed with therapy. The therapist orients the client about what will happen during therapy, how often they will attend, what a session looks like, what homework needs to be done. They will try out a few tasks, such as diary-keeping, to see whether the client is willing and able to work in a DBT way. This emphasis on commitment and motivation is necessary to reduce drop-out and failure experiences and build a high level of commitment before starting therapy.

Once a contract is agreed, therapy involves individual sessions where the client and therapist work together through a list of 'target behaviours'. These include life-threatening, therapy-interfering and quality-of-life interfering behaviours. The client arrives at the session with a completed diary. If a target behaviour (e.g. gambling) has occurred, a behavioural analysis ('chain analysis') is carried out and the function of the behaviour identified. A plan is made as to what the client could do differently next time an urge to carry out the behaviour appears. The client attends group sessions where she or he learns new skills to replace the old maladaptive coping behaviours. These include mindfulness, crisis survival, emotional regulation, interpersonal and self-management skills.

The DBT therapist offers coaching between sessions to help clients use new skills instead of problem behaviours. Therapists belong to peer supervision groups ('consult groups'), where they receive DBT-style support to manage their own behaviours so they can stay effective.

The effectiveness of DBT

There is an impressive body of evidence that DBT is effective with a range of presentations including suicide, self-harm, eating disorders, substance misuse, addictions and more (e.g., Lynch, 2018).

Suggested further reading

Swales, M. A. & Heard, H. L. (2016). *Dialectical Behaviour Therapy (The CBT Distinctive Features Series)*. London: Routledge.

References

Linehan, M. M., Komtois, K., Murray, A., Brown, M., Gallup, R. et al. (2006). Two-year randomized controlled trial and follow-up of dialectical behavior therapy vs therapy by experts for suicidal behaviors and borderline personality disorder. *Archives of General Psychiatry*, *63*(7), 757–766.

Lynch, T. (2018). *Radically Open Dialectical Behavior Therapy: Theory and Practice for Treating Disorders of Overcontrol*, Oakland, CA: New Harbinger.

5

CFT in a nutshell

What is CFT?

Compassion focused therapy (CFT) was developed by Paul Gilbert and colleagues (e.g. Gilbert, 2014). It integrates cognitive behavioural therapy (CBT) with concepts from evolutionary psychology, social psychology, developmental psychology, Buddhist psychology and neuroscience. Techniques from CBT are integrated with techniques to increase the client's capacity for and practice of compassion and self-compassion. CFT is particularly useful when working with people with severe and enduring mental health problems, many of whom have high levels of shame and self-criticism and who have difficulty in feeling warmth toward, and being kind to, themselves or others.

How CFT conceptualises psychological distress

Shame and self-criticism often underlie anxiety, depression, eating disorders, personality disorders and psychosis, to name but a few. Problems with shame and self-criticism are often rooted in a history of abuse, bullying, neglect and lack of affection in the family.

Biological evolution informs CFT's theory of psychological distress. Two key concepts are, first, that humans have 'old brains', roughly coterminous with the limbic system or midbrain, where emotions are generated. Second, 'new brains', which evolved later, do the thinking, planning and ruminating. These two systems interact and yet are not entirely well connected. Our old brain can 'hijack' the best laid plans of our new brains and make us behave in unhelpful, primitive ways. Also, our new brain can overthink threat, for example, and stimulate extreme emotional reactions in our old brains. A second key concept is that humans have evolved with at least three primal types of emotion regulation systems:

- The threat (protection) system
- The drive (resource-seeking) system
- The soothing (affiliation) system

CFT emphasises the links between cognitive and behavioural patterns and these three emotion regulation systems. Anxiety and anger are usually experienced when the *threat* system is triggered. Excitement and interest are characteristic when the *drive* system is uppermost. Contentment and caring are uppermost when the *soothing* system is activated. Kindness is seen as an evolved capacity to care for others and for ourselves, and as a useful capacity to develop through therapy.

Developmental psychology recognises that high levels of shame and self-criticism are often rooted in childhood following experiences of abuse, bullying, neglect, lack of affection, etc. These experiences can damage development, which in turn can lead on to long-term problems (see Chapter 11). Dysfunctional relationships in childhood are often mirrored in adult relationships. Survivors of abuse generally have an overactive threat system learned in childhood. For example, a child with a controlling, abusive or aggressive parent may grow up to be submissive (so as not to provoke the parent) or aggressive and controlling (so as to avoid being a victim).

Buddhist psychology contributes compassion to the CFT mix. The Dalai Lama described compassion as a sensitivity to suffering in self and others, with a commitment to try to alleviate and prevent it. The idea of generating compassion to alleviate distress is central to Buddhism. Compassion requires mindfulness, defined as the ability to pay attention to the present moment, in a non-judgemental manner, with compassion. Mindfulness skills allow us to focus our attention where we want it to be, rather than being pulled off course by strong (evolved) emotions and other distractions.

Social psychology emphasises the social context in which we exist and how we perceive ourselves in this context. Our self-concepts are determined by our interactions with other people and social systems on many levels, affecting our mood, behaviour, thoughts and physiology. Interacting with compassion can change the way other people see us and the way we see the world.

In terms of neuroscience, CFT recognises that the nervous system has both arousal and soothing systems, involving the sympathetic and parasympathetic nervous systems. These systems determine our feelings and ways of relating to others and the world. This takes us back to the three drive systems mentioned earlier: threat, resource-seeking and soothing. People with overstimulated threat systems may be continually on the lookout for threat, highly reactive to triggers and likely to be highly anxious or aggressive. People with overstimulated resource-seeking drive systems may be prone to risk-taking or addictive behaviours. Clients can learn to manage each system using compassionate mind training and respond differently to life situations.

How does CFT help us to change?

Change in CFT starts with psychoeducation. The client is given information about our complex and difficult brains, the old and new brain systems. This concept is used to begin the process of compassionate understanding of our self, our emotions and our thinking minds. Our old brains can 'hijack' our new brains so that we behave in emotionally driven, often unhelpful ways. The point is made that we did not choose to be the way we are, we are a product of evolution and our own personal learning histories. It is not our fault that we are the way we are. However, we can learn to stand back and observe this process happening, using mindfulness skills to direct our attention where we want it to be, rather than where our emotions are dragging us. Further education is given about the function of emotions, and how they link into the three drive systems. Emotions are often felt first in the body, as hard-wired or as learned responses, and we cannot prevent these reactions happening as they are natural.

25

The central therapeutic technique of CFT is compassionate mind training, which teaches the skills and attributes of compassion. Compassionate mind training helps transform problematic patterns of cognition and emotion and develop new self–self and self–other relationships. CFT recognises that compassion 'flows' in three directions: compassion we can feel for another or others, compassion we can feel from others to ourselves, and compassion we can direct towards ourselves (self-compassion). We can shift from blaming ourselves to being curious about how our minds work, helping us to be open to and tolerant of distress.

In order to develop compassionate mind skills, we must practice cultivating compassion. These practices include attention training, soothing rhythm breathing, safe place imagery, compassionate self-cultivation, compassionate-self focusing and compassionate image focusing. The 'Perfect Nurturer' image, developed by Deborah Lee (2005), involves creating an image of a person, spirit, animal or plant that can be relied upon to give compassionate validation if needed.

The effectiveness of CFT

A recent meta-analysis showed that CFT is a promising intervention for people with problems involving shame and self-criticism (Leaviss & Uttley, 2015). To date, CFT has a smaller body of evidence than the other therapies in this book, but this is growing (Gilbert, 2014).

Suggested further reading

Gilbert, P. (2010). *Compassion Focused Therapy. The CBT Distinctive Features Series*. London: Routledge.

References

Gilbert, P. (2014). The origins and nature of compassion focused therapy. *British Journal of Clinical Psychology*, *53*(1), 6–41.

Leaviss, L. & Uttley, L. (2015). Psychotherapeutic benefits of compassion-focused therapy: An early systematic review. *Psychological Medicine*, *45*(5), 927–994.

Lee, D. A. (2005). The perfect nurturer: A model to develop a compassionate mind within the context of cognitive therapy. In P. Gilbert (Ed.), *Compassion: Conceptualisations, Research and Use in Psychotherapy*, 326–351. London: Brunner-Routledge.

6

Why integrate CBT and third wave approaches?

This chapter considers the desirable qualities of an integrated therapy. Then we look at the pros and cons of taking an integrated approach.

What does a good integrated therapy look like?

The term 'integrated therapy' refers to approaches combining theory and practice from several different evidence-based therapies. An integrated approach should be *coherent*, in that it makes sense to the client and the therapist, and be theoretically robust, having clear underlying principles. It should also draw only from evidence-based therapies. Our version, CBT+, is described in this book and also in the self-help book *Get Your Life Back: The Most Effective Therapies for a Better You.* CBT+ combines CBT, ACT, DBT and CFT, using a radical behavioural perspective to integrate understanding and techniques. It is only one example of the many possibilities.

Protocol vs. principle

Some therapeutic approaches involve protocols that can be fairly prescriptive accounts of what to do and when. Alternatively, many therapists find working from principle most helpful, as each case is unique. This tension can be seen quite clearly in CBT. The principles of the therapy involve developing a therapeutic alliance. We should set off on a shared Socratically curious journey, where therapist and client investigate the accuracy and the consequences of the client's thinking, feeling and behaving patterns. CBT has protocols for most disorders; the extensive evidence base is built on research using presentations selected to fit with specific diagnostic criteria and using therapists who stick to specific protocols for treating that disorder. However, in the uncontrolled world of real life, people come along with varied and wonderful presentations.

Let us introduce Khalil, an experienced CBT therapist familiar with the many protocols that CBT offers. He meets our client Rengina. At first he decides Rengina has a history of being bullied at school and has become socially anxious. He looks up the diagnostic criteria for social anxiety and decides to use a CBT approach based on a well-known model of social anxiety. But then he observes that Rengina is having significant panic attacks with phobic avoidance of the bus stop. She worries about her mental and physical health and has episodes of depersonalisation. She was dependent on her mother, and behaves in the same way towards her therapist. Should Khalil adapt the social anxiety model to include all of these phenomena? Or should Khalil go with multiple diagnoses and protocols? Perhaps it would be better to make a bespoke CBT formulation (e.g. Persons, Roberts & Zalecki, 2006) concerning the development and maintenance of the problems and work from there. Khalil could then apply the principles of CBT and tailor the assessment and approach to Rengina's presentation. These dilemmas exist across therapies, but especially in CBT, where there are so many evidence-based models. Our offering, CBT+, is a principle-based approach, where the therapist's task is to guide the client through various change processes. We suggest NAVIGATES (Chapters 21–29) not as a prescriptive protocol but as a guide as to how to proceed.

Is combining therapies a good idea?

There are of course pros and cons of combining therapies. Some pros of combining different therapies include:

- Most of us attend training in several therapies at different levels, absorbing new theories and practical skills, and we go on to use them in our practice
- It is better to have a thought-through, consistent approach rather than an ad hoc, reactive one, which might happen if we randomly apply our knowledge in the moment
- We have a duty to our clients to deliver the best possible interventions
- No one therapeutic approach has all the answers – the field is still in its infancy
- Focusing on the processes of therapeutic change and how to facilitate them with our clients allows us to think, work and research trans-diagnostically and trans-therapeutically

But here are some cons:

- We may lose the theoretical 'tightness' needed to effectively formulate cases and design interventions
- Theories underpinning different approaches may be fundamentally incompatible or clash in significant areas
- We may lose track of what we are doing and why as we go along, as things get too complex
- We may not be able to guarantee the effectiveness of our intervention: although each therapy has an evidence base, new integrations may not themselves have been tested
- We may have to start all over again, researching the effectiveness of a new approach, or of many different approaches that each integrate therapies in different and unique ways

One approach to pros and cons is to hold them in our minds as a dialectic; that is, as apparent contradictions that we assume will have a synthesis if we seek it. For now, we suggest the DBT strategy of 'entering the paradox', that is, to observe the apparent opposites and simply hold them in mind.

When and with whom should we apply an integrated approach?

Is it the case that if we have the skills and knowledge, we should use everything we have got, wherever we got it from, in the interests of delivering the best possible service, so long as we have a good formulation?

Or is it the case that certain presentations are best addressed by well-established protocols? In the UK, IAPT (Improving Access to Psychological Therapies) has clear approaches to anxiety and depression. Clark and colleagues (e.g. Williams et al., 2016) strongly advise IAPT therapists to categorise a given presentation and then adhere to the NICE (National Institute for Clinical Excellence) recommended intervention. Evidence from the IAPT database suggests that outcomes based on symptom reduction are much better when this is done.

The complexity and severity of a presentation may make therapists more likely to switch approaches. Often CBT therapists will begin with 'standard' CBT, moving on to working at the level of core beliefs if standard CBT is ineffective. They may then recommend or switch to other therapeutic models such as ACT, DBT or CFT if all else has failed. This kind of client journey can mean repeated failure experiences for both clients and therapists. Perhaps an integrated therapeutic approach can offer a kinder, more effective and more efficient alternative.

References

Persons, J. B., Roberts, N. A., & Zalecki, C. A. (2006). Naturalistic outcome of case formulation-driven cognitive-behavior therapy for anxious depressed outpatients. *Behaviour Research and Therapy*, *44*(7), 1041–1051.

Williams, R., Farquharson, L., Palmer, L., Bassett, P., Clarke, J. et al. (2016). Patient preference in psychological treatment and associations with self-reported outcome: National cross-sectional survey in England and Wales. *BMC Psychiatry*, *16*(4), 1–8.

Behaviour theory and philosophy

This chapter looks at the theory and philosophies underlying different therapeutic approaches, to show what we have incorporated into CBT+.

A bit of history

Since the days of Freudians, Jungians and Kleinians, leading figures have competed for their share of therapist loyalties. In recent years there has been a real paradigm shift, with the requirement for evidence-based theory and practice. This requirement for a scientific approach is enshrined in institutions such as NICE (the UK National Institute for Clinical Excellence). Behaviour therapies were among the first therapies to place value on the scientific approach. They emphasised the need to operationalise concepts: aggression, for example, cannot be observed, whilst smacking a person across the face certainly can be. By focusing on the observable and measurable, behaviourists could claim to be acting in the scientific tradition. Extensive experimental work with animals gave us the principles of learning and behaviour change that we still work with today. It is these principles in their modern form that can provide the base on which to build integrated approaches.

The cognitive therapy movement began with the problem of 'rule-governed behaviour'. If I think that the rule is that I get rewarded for shaking my head, when really my finger-tapping is the target behaviour, my head shaking will increase! Rats, of course, do not suffer from this problem. The importance of language and thinking cannot be ignored. Skinner's perceived failure to account for language within a behavioural framework led to a rejection of behavioural principles.

Cognitive science was soon embraced as the key knowledge base. Studies of information processing relevant to clinical work include selective attention and memory, subliminal perception and the way threatening material affects these processes. At the same time, relational frame theory (Hayes, Barnes-Holmes & Roche, 2013) emerged as a behavioural account of human language and thought and now underpins the work of ACT therapists. It accounts for the rapidity with which we learn relationships between concepts, without the need for such learning to be directly reinforced.

Alongside all of this, evolutionary psychology has played a major role in our understanding of emotions and behaviour. The basic drives for survival, attachment and achievement have helped us understand the power of feelings and emotion-driven action.

In December 1903, American psychologist William James invited Anagarika Dharmapala to lecture at Harvard University. After the lecture on Buddhism, James remarked, 'This is the psychology everybody will be studying 25 years from now'. The idea of release from dissatisfaction through mindfulness and acceptance practices has now become central to many therapies.

A bit of theory

The philosopher S. C. Pepper (1942) discussed the problem that we can never observe the world directly, but must always be interpreting our experience. He outlined four 'World Hypotheses' (world views or conceptual systems): formism, mechanism, contextualism and organicism. Mechanism holds that we can explain things by analysing their parts: just as we can understand a steam engine by taking it apart and then reassembling it, human behaviour can eventually be explained by finding the basic ingredients (thoughts, feelings, behaviour and body sensations, for example). Contextualism holds that everything is relative and that behaviour can only be understood in terms of its context. If you see a man dead in a field, the mechanistic explanation could be that he had a heart attack. The contextualist explanation is that he ran away from a bull, thus over stressing his body and causing a heart attack, as he was rather unfit. Both explanations would be accepted as 'true' in our culture, but each gives a different quality of knowledge. Cognitive theory and CBT could be seen as an examples of mechanism, in that they attempt to unpack the fine details of how our minds function. This may be an unfair analysis, though, as CBT pays attention to the environment and setting conditions where behaviours occur. ACT and DBT explicitly identify themselves as based on contextualist theories.

One type of contextualist theory is structuralism. Structuralist theories are theories that propose an underlying, invisible 'deep structure'. This structure determines what gets manifested at the surface. Cognitive therapists talk about core beliefs or schemas, underlying assumptions and negative automatic thoughts, often represented as a triangle. Core beliefs are the deep structure level of personality and information processing. They are often learned early in development and are hard to change. In this sense we could say that CBT has elements of contextualisim as well as mechanism. ACT therapists speak about 'relational frames': deep structures that determine how we learn about and experience the world through language. CFT therapists have the concept of drives as deep structures, evolved to make human beings successful in the world. DBT does not seem to have a deep structure concept, although the principles of behaviour theory and dialectical philosophy are its basis.

One thing all these approaches, and others, have in common, is an acceptance of behavioural theory. Positive and negative reinforcement and punishment, as well as paired associate learning, are central concepts when explaining people's learning histories. Contingency management and exposure are key techniques for producing change.

Another thing in common is the application of acceptance techniques (derived from Buddhism) to the management of the conscious mind. These techniques help us to develop an 'observing self' or 'wise mind', separate from the 'thinking' and the 'emotional' selves. Becoming able to label and manage emotional states, identify the direction one would like to take in life and make conscious choices as to what to do next are all essential skills for positive therapeutic progress.

How CBT+ puts all this together

In terms of theory, CBT+ embraces the behavioural and cognitive theories described above. Philosophically we identify CBT+ as a contextualist therapy.

Within this context, we believe that an integrated therapy should identify and focus on the core processes that are needed to facilitate positive change. This is a principle examined in detail in Hayes and Hofmann (2018), and to a lesser extent in the following chapters.

Practically speaking, CBT+ begins with acceptance: naming the client's problems (target behaviours) and strengths using extensive validation with the client and beginning to model a mindful, non-judgemental approach to this. Commitment work may be necessary to build motivation before beginning any change work. Formulation of core beliefs, underlying assumptions and negative automatic thoughts combines with describing the overall maintenance cycles that keep problem behaviours going. CBT+ continues by identifying the client's values and preferred life directions. Then a two-pronged approach works on reducing target behaviours and increasing steps towards valued living. Metaphors and strategies from all four therapies are used to achieve this.

References

Hayes, S. C., Barnes-Holmes, D., & Roche, B. (Eds.). (2013). *Relational Frame Theory: A Post-Skinnerian Account of Human Language and Cognition*. New York: Springer.

Hayes, S. C. & Hofmann, S. G. (2018). *Processed-Based CBT: The Science and Core Clinical Competencies of Cognitive Behavioral Therapy*. California, CA: New Harbinger Publications.

Pepper, S. C. (1942). *World Hypotheses: A Study in Evidence*. Berkeley, CA: University of California Press.

8

Core processes of change 1

Trust, commitment and compassion

Maladaptive coping, rumination and self-blame

Peter Kinderman and his colleagues (2013) studied 32,827 (aged 18–85 years) self-selected respondents from the general population who completed an open access online battery of questionnaires hosted by the BBC. A family history of mental health difficulties, social deprivation and traumatic or abusive life experiences all strongly predicted higher levels of anxiety and depression. However, these relationships were mediated by psychological processes: specifically lack of adaptive coping (usually involving avoidant coping), rumination and self-blame. These three psychological processes are each amenable to change through therapy. Adaptive coping skills can be taught, rumination addressed and self-blame ameliorated. Avoidant coping, rumination and self-blame all involve lack of acceptance and lack of compassion, the opposite of mindfulness skills.

In order to address rumination, we can learn first to identify and then to handle our thoughts and feelings in new, more compassionate and mindful ways. We can learn to 'turn the mind' *away* from rumination. We can learn skills to turn the mind *towards* values and goals. We can use cognitive restructuring to curiously question and explore our thoughts and come up with new perspectives.

In order to address self-blame, we can firstly understand where this comes from, then notice the effects of self-bullying, and finally learn new skills, daring to be compassionate and kind to ourselves and to others.

To tackle avoidant coping, we can practice willing acceptance and deliberately decide to approach feared situations and experiences or 'make room for' negative emotions. We can learn skills to self-soothe, survive crises and act mindfully to help us do this.

The core processes of change

This chapter lays out some of the core processes of change needed for successful therapy, namely trust, commitment and compassion. Mindfulness permeates each of these processes and is a central tool used by the therapist and learned by the client.

Trust

It is impossible to separate building trust from building commitment in therapy; these two processes must occur in tandem. If there is damaged attachment produced by adversity, abuse and neglect, this can continue into adulthood. It can be counteracted through developing a sincerely committed and trusting relationship between therapist and client. Even without damage caused by adversity, any work between a therapist and client needs a basis of trust and therapeutic alliance.

One metaphor for the therapist stance is to be a rock in the middle of a sea, which is sometimes calm and sometimes stormy, as the client's anxiety produces variations in trust and commitment levels. Of course, we are not rocks, and can be swayed by our client's reactions and lack of progress, so that the need for therapist support is paramount. The DBT-style consult group is a good model for peer support and supervision (Linehan, 1993). Another element of DBT is that the therapist should take a dialectical stance (Linehan, 1993). This means that instead of persuading, lecturing or arguing with our clients, we practice radical acceptance and look for the context that gives meaning and understandability to the client's behaviour.

By building trust, we create a space where the client can enter an affiliative, safe state of body and mind. Gilbert and Choden (2014) argue that this is the basic drive state of safety and contentment, in which new learning can occur. Lastly, by building mutual trust, we create the context for facilitating change. The client will be motivated to seek our acceptance and approval and will value our guidance. Because the client becomes attached to us, we can use our approval and disapproval judiciously and gently to positively reinforce adaptive behaviour and to reduce the occurrence of mal-adaptive behaviour (contingency management).

Building trust is an ongoing process throughout therapy and requires genuine sincerity and validation skills from the therapist along with an ability to confront when necessary. We should be prepared to be imperfect and admit mistakes or unhelpful behaviour on our own parts. Crises of trust in the relationship should be named and addressed directly. Overcoming these crises together provides vital new learning for clients who may have assumed that every relationship breach is final.

Commitment

Ambivalence towards change may come from a variety of sources. There may be a long history of failure and hopelessness, for example for those diagnosed with personality disorder and/or having revolving door inpatient stays. The very act of committing to therapy involves engaging with wanting something, and so risking failure and despair.

The first stage of building commitment is for the client to experience the therapist's mindful acceptance of the client's current presentation, balanced with optimism about their ability to change. Offering genuine choice on both the therapist's and client's parts, changes the process. The client is faced with making an *active* choice to proceed, after being informed of what exactly is expected of them and of the therapist.

During the pre-therapy commitment phase in DBT and in CBT+, three strands of work take place. The first is orienting the client, giving her information about the therapy, frequency of meetings, between-session assignments, etc. The second is the use of commitment techniques or 'strategies' (from DBT) to increase levels of commitment. The third is to assess the client's ability to do the therapy. Can the client read? Can they complete between-session assignments? Can they complete a diary?

This is the best phase of therapy for drop out to occur, as we have not officially started so there can be no failure for either party. Few resources have been expended on each side. We are maximising our chances of progress once commitment is agreed and a contract made.

Compassion

Compassion can be seen as having two elements: empathy (for self or other) and the ability to act on that empathy (Gilbert & Choden, 2014). It is easier for clients with extreme self-blame, shame and self-loathing to start with showing compassion for other people and then to move towards applying the same thing to themselves. Clients often rephrase self-compassion as 'feeling sorry for myself' and other terms implying this is a self-indulgence or selfishness. Therapists should embody compassion in their work with clients as well as demonstrating the difference between selfishness and self-care. Defusion techniques (separating the self from one's thoughts, from ACT) as well as cognitive restructuring at the schema level (from CBT) can help increase compassionate thinking, whilst compassionate mind training, two chair work and the 'Perfect Nurturer' from CFT work at a more directly emotional level (see Chapter 5).

The chapters in Part II describe practical techniques and strategies from the four therapies to help us build trust, commitment and compassion.

References

Gilbert, P. & Choden. (2014). *Mindful Compassion: How the Science of Compassion Can Help You Understand Your Emotions, Live in the Present, and Connect Deeply with Others*. London: Robinson.

Kinderman, P., Schwannauer, M., Pontin, P., & Tai, S. (2013). Psychological processes mediate the impact of familial risk, social circumstances and life events on mental health. *PLoS One, 8*(10), e76564.

Linehan, M. M. (1993). *Cognitive Behavioral Treatment of Borderline Personality Disorder*. New York: Guilford Press.

9

Core processes of change 2

Perspective taking, exposure and learning new skills

In this chapter we look at more core processes of change, the importance of being able to stand back and observe (perspective taking), approach behaviours (exposure) and the acquisition of new practical skills in several areas: emotional regulation, relationship management and mindfulness.

Perspective taking

Perspective taking involves the central act of finding new meanings. The four therapeutic approaches we are concerned with, CBT, ACT, DBT and CFT, each have procedures to develop what we can call an 'observing self'. A metaphor for this might be that, instead of being the hamster running inside the wheel, we can stand back and, first, watch ourselves running, second, choose to get off the wheel and third, decide not to get on the wheel in the first place. As we get better and better at taking a non-judgemental observer perspective, each of these things becomes possible.

In CBT the therapist sits with the client and may review a thought record. Just the act of making this record puts the client in an observer position, separate from their thoughts. From here the client can begin to notice how feelings are 'attached' to thoughts. Together the client and therapist can test out different perspectives on the situations where the thoughts have arisen and experiment with the consequences of looking at things differently. Socratic questioning is a specific technique designed to promote perspective taking. In mindfulness-based CBT (Keng, Smoski & Robins, 2011), mindfulness skills are explicitly brought in to provide an alternative to engaging with thoughts as if they are true.

In ACT the stated aim is not to change thoughts but to change the person's *relationship* with the thoughts. The observing self can see that some thoughts are unhelpful (not in line with preferred values), and simply mindfully leave them be. The aim is to carry the thoughts along in life as if they were passengers on the bus that the client is driving. Paradoxically, this often leads to thoughts changing. This is done by teaching a new focus on identified values rather than moment to moment internal experience. In DBT there is less emphasis on thoughts and more on behaviours, although thought challenging is included in the DBT skills manual (Linehan, 2014). Having unhelpful thoughts of various kinds could be listed in DBT as target behaviours to reduce and so become the focus of change in this way. For example, having (and agreeing with) the thought 'I cannot possibly sit in a group' would be framed as a behaviour to reduce, because it interferes with participating in skills groups. In CFT the focus is back onto changing thoughts, through explaining that we are all the products of evolution and therefore it is *not our fault* that we have powerful emotions and drives. CFT also focuses on inducing new compassionate states of mind through compassionate mind training, including thinking new compassionate thoughts about others and ourselves.

Each therapy, then, focuses on changing either thoughts themselves, our relationship to them or both of these, and does this largely through inducing perspective taking.

CBT+ uses perspective taking to both review internal experiences like thoughts and images *and* change our relationship to them. Two metaphors we use are of 'helicoptering up' and looking down on a situation from a new perspective (from CBT and CFT), and of thoughts and feelings as 'untrained puppies' in the 'yards' of our minds. The aim of perspective taking is to become aware of these puppies and train them to come along with us on a lead as we decide how to live our lives (from ACT and DBT).

Exposure

When we speak of exposure in training settings or at conferences, we sometimes meet with the reaction 'We know all this' from the therapists attending. Although this may seem a well-worn topic, it remains incompletely understood, especially in terms of the psychological mechanisms through which it works, and exactly how to use exposure. The central principle is of course to reduce avoidance and increase willing experiencing. We know for sure that if we can pull this off, our clients will free themselves from much suffering.

From cognitive and behavioural theories, we have important concepts about how to go about using exposure in therapy. Many of these are based on the idea that exposure works through habituation. Foa and Rothbaum's (1998) protocol for reliving, for example, requires the client to record their account of a trauma and listen to the recording repeatedly until the emotional responses diminish.

The work of Salkovskis and his colleagues has been seminal in introducing the concept of 'safety behaviours' (Salkovskis et al., 1999). These are responses that somehow protect a person from fully experiencing an emotion such as fear, and thus prevent exposure. For example, Rengina might count in her head during an exposure therapy session. Cognitive and behavioural avoidance also prevent exposure. It is often considered essential to prevent such behaviours during exposure work.

The practice of graded exposure has emerged, where increasingly challenging situations are used to produce exposure. In addition, SUDs (subjective units of distress) reported by the client are used during exposure procedures, to ensure there is sufficient exposure (say, 7 or more out of 10) but not too much (say, 10 out of 10).

Morris (2017), however, cites evidence that exposure protocols work even when SUDs do not reduce during exposure. This implies that the mechanism may in fact be new learning, for example 'this situation is no longer dangerous', rather than habituation. In ACT terms, exposure involves the formation of new 'relational frames'.

In any case, exposure work is central to CBT+. Re-living and re-scripting work is included (see Chapters 15 and 27). In addition, the therapist frequently asks the client 'would you be willing to … ?', creating the conditions for spontaneous exposure to occur. The therapist models willingness to experience difficult emotions through his/her own behaviour in the session. For example, the therapist might share 'It's difficult to bring this up, but we need to discuss what happens when you get angry with me'.

Learning new skills

The direct teaching of new skills and new understanding is very effectively done in group settings. This allows us to use peer support and peer pressure as well as to build mini communities of clients with shared struggles. The *DBT Skills Training Manual* (Linehan, 2014) and other authors' interpretations of DBT skills (e.g., Pederson, 2017) have borrowed widely from CBT, ACT and CFT and so we find it difficult to improve on such an extensive collection of concepts and group exercises and activities. We recommend CBT+ be run alongside a DBT skills group or individual sessions on DBT skills teaching, to maximise the chances of the client learning all the skills needed for change. The more complex the presentation, the more benefit this will bring.

In individual CBT+ therapy, we actively teach new skills in session, as well as setting assignments for the client to complete between sessions. These assignments will either help generalise a skill learned in session or contribute to learning a new skill outside of session.

Emotion regulation, crisis survival, mindfulness and interpersonal skills are the categories used in DBT skills group teaching. These same skills are emphasised in CBT+, although the therapist may draw from any of the four therapies to achieve the desired outcome. This is so that the client becomes able to experience and manage intense emotions, get through crisis times without self or other destruction, and manage their relationships with others. We also add skills for the self–self relationship, such as compassionate mind training.

References

Foa, E. B. & Rothbaum, B. A. (1998). *Treating the Trauma of Rape: Cognitive Behavioral Therapy for PTSD*. New York: Guilford Press.

Keng, S.-L., Smoski, M. J., & Robins, C. J. (2011). Effects of mindfulness on psychological health: A review of empirical studies. *Clinical Psychology Review*, *31*(6), 1041–1056.

Linehan, M. M. (2014). *DBT Skills Training Manual*, 2nd Edition. New York: Guilford Press.

Morris, E. (2017). So long to SUDS: Exposure is not about fear reduction … it's about new learning and flexibility. *CBT Today*, February, 210–211.

Pederson, L. (2017). *The Expanded Dialectical Behavior Therapy Skills Manual: DBT for Self-Help and Individual and Group Treatment Settings*. Eau Claire, WI: Pesipub & Media.

Salkovskis, P. M., Clark, D. M., Hackmann, A., Wells, A. G., & Gelder, M. G. (1999). An experimental investigation of the role of safety-seeking behaviours in the maintenance of panic disorder with agoraphobia. *Behaviour Research and Therapy*, *37*(60), 559–574.

10

Principles and protocol for CBT+

NAVIGATES

This chapter presents the idea of principles versus protocol in therapeutic practice and then introduces the NAVIGATES acronym as an aid to practising CBT+.

Therapeutic principles and protocol

The focus in this book so far has been on therapeutic *principles* and the discussion of core processes of change, including:

- The fundamental stance of acceptance by the therapist
- The importance of formulation as a means of understanding the client's presentation and deciding how to proceed
- The need for attachment and a high-quality relationship between therapist and client
- The behavioural principles underlying the approach

The second half of the book focuses on the practicalities of making all this happen. It is structured around the acronym NAVIGATES, which describes a *protocol*, or suggested procedure, for conducting CBT+.

The dialectic here is that the protocol itself is intended to be very flexible and open to modification and change. It is not necessary to proceed in a simple linear fashion. The process of therapy needs to change in response to emerging information and changing circumstances in the client's life, the outside world and the therapeutic

Table 10.1 The NAVIGATES protocol

N	Name the problem behaviour(s), work towards doing this without judgements (mindfully) and reframe
A	Increase Awareness of thoughts, feelings, body sensations, behaviour and Acceptance of these
V	Validate the client's current pain in terms of past learning (formulating the development of the problem) Values – clarify the client's values
I	Identify the function of the behaviour and plan to do something different (formulating and targeting which behaviours to reduce)
G	Goals – agree some small goals to move the client towards identified values (increasing agency and behavioural repertoire)
A	Accept self and others (deeper work on self and other schemas, compassion, reducing self-loathing and perfectionism)
T	Tackle Trauma (having prepared or 'stabilised' the client decide to what extent and how any past trauma should be directly approached)
E	Emotions and Exposure – learn to identify, experience and regulate emotions (this aspect runs throughout the work)
S	Skills training – learn to handle thoughts, urges, flashbacks, images, etc. (this aspect also runs throughout the work and may be complemented with group skills training or individual skills training)

relationship. We advise using this protocol with an awareness of this flexibility. For example, checking through Table 10.1 throughout the therapy, the therapist might ask 'have we addressed this aspect yet – do I need to revisit the formulation, or teach a new skill?'

The importance of first motivating and committing the client to therapy is outlined in the next part of this book. The NAVIGATES acronym assumes the therapist has at least the client's active and informed consent and willingness to proceed with therapy.

The second half of this book devotes a chapter to each of the NAVIGATES aspects, exploring how the therapist can practically include each in a coherent therapeutic journey.

Ways to use the NAVIGATES protocol

The self-help book *Get Your Life Back: The Most Effective Therapies for a Better You* is intended as a companion book to the present volume. Using both together, the therapist may assign reading and exercises from that book as between-session assignments. Shortlisted for the British Medical Association's Popular Medicine Book of the Year, 2018, *Get Your Life Back* takes clients through a process of naming and building awareness of their problem(s) non-judgementally; other chapters develop mindfulness and show how to clarify values and set goals. Later the book shows how problem behaviours 'work' in terms of short-term gain and long-term pain and how to plan to break out of the identified patterns. Self-validation and self-acceptance come next, along with (limited) advice about handling the effects of trauma. The book advises seeking expert help for significant trauma work. Skills for identifying and handling thoughts, feelings, physiological reactions and behaviour are taught throughout the book using techniques from CBT, DBT, ACT and CFT. Lastly, the book addresses the need for persistence, overcoming setbacks and being imperfect. The website www.getyourlifeback.global contains free downloadable exercises, handouts and diaries that can be used throughout the NAVIGATES protocol.

The present volume can of course stand alone, but can also be used in conjunction with *Get Your Life Back* and/or with handouts from the book to assist therapist and client in their work together. Please read on for more practical and concrete examples of the integrated CBT+ approach.

Suggested further reading

Kennedy, F. & Pearson, D. (2017). *Get Your Life Back. The Most Effective Therapies for a Better You*. London: Robinson.

11

Early trauma experiences and adult problems

Why do early experiences continue to be a problem for adults?

Many problems seem to stem from childhood, following abuse neglect, loss or other adversity. Such childhood experiences can become part of adult problems, entwined into our lives. Childhood is a time of rapid development and change. Developmental steps or skills have to be mastered in the right order and preferably at the right time. Trauma or adversity during childhood can adversely affect development, leading to problems with cognitive, affective and behavioural regulation. There can be negative effects on the person's self-esteem, interactions with others and experience of the world.

Evidence that mild early experiences of adversity can increase resilience should not be confused with the damaging effects of more severe adversity that is dealt with in therapy (Seery, 2011). CBT+ aims to build on resilience and deal with the typical patterns found in survivors of abuse and neglect.

The research

Adversity can be defined as sexual and physical abuse, poor nutrition, high levels of stress, abandonment, witnessing domestic violence, dysfunctional parenting, neglect, bullying, living in war zones, poverty and parental mental health problems (Read & Bentall, 2010).

The prevalence of adversity should not be underestimated. The Adverse Childhood Experiences (ACE) study (Felitti et al., 1998) included 17,337 people: 30 % reported physical abuse; 19.9% sexual abuse; 23.5% reported being exposed to family alcohol abuse; 18.8% to mental illness; 12.5% witnessed their mothers being physically attacked; and 4.9% reported family drug abuse.

There is a strong and growing body of evidence linking adversity in childhood with adult mental health problems. Kessler et al. (2010) reviewed studies using data from 52,000 participants in 21 countries. They concluded the link was irrefutable. In addition, the ACE study demonstrated powerful links to a great variety of physical health problems and early death.

The psychological processes mediating the relationship between childhood adversity and problems in adulthood were investigated by Kinderman et al. (2013). They identified *rumination, self-blame* and *lack of adaptive coping* as mediators. In practical terms for therapy, it may be useful to think of these as rumination, self-loathing and avoidant coping.

Post-traumatic stress disorder (PTSD)

The signs of PTSD in adults and children are clustered into re-living (flashbacks, nightmares), avoidance, arousal and negative cognitions (American Psychiatric Association, 2013). The interaction between such symptoms and the demands of parents, friends, school and study can be such that a vicious circle of problems develops. For example, extreme angry outbursts can result in school exclusion, ruptures in family relationships and the beginnings of the self-loathing found in the Kinderman study mentioned earlier. Complex PTSD is included for the first time in the *Diagnostic and Statistical Manual of Mental Disorders V* and is a description of the extensive problems resulting from the interactions between childhood PTSD, developmental processes and environmental responses.

Attachment

At birth, a baby must attach to carers. As the child grows, she or he learns confidence and tolerates being some distance away from carers. A young child will move away perhaps a metre or so, keeping the carer in view at all times. Any further and *separation anxiety* will kick in and the child will move back into the safety zone. This developmental process slowly builds a sense of security, an understanding of the world and of relationships. Without the presence of a reliable carer, the child may be in a constant state of separation anxiety and unable to self-soothe. Normal attachment is impossible and clingy, detached or disordered attachment results, with high levels of anxiety. Abuse by a carer is very damaging as it creates conflict between our basic drives to keep safe and to attach. This can result in a fragmented sense of self. The child may develop with one self-state activated during interaction with the carer when the carer is safe and another self-state when the carer is dangerous. Dissociated self-states are characteristic of borderline personality disorder (BPD) and dissociative identity disorder (DID) (Kennedy, 2013; Van der Hart & Steele, 2013).

Sensitive periods and developmental collapse

For each developmental task, children are geared up to develop super fast for a short time only. These times are known as sensitive periods. It is much more difficult to develop a skill (e.g., managing anxiety and controlling impulses) if the sensitive period is missed because of adversity. A child kept in a cot with minimal carer contact in an orphanage will not learn to take a first step during the sensitive period for managing anxiety. Later, placed in a loving family, learning will be slower as the sensitive period for managing anxiety has passed by. Also, there will be sensitive periods for current skills, such as controlling impulses, which are now happening in competition with the 'catch up' task of managing anxiety.

Development builds skills, like blocks, one 'on top' of the other. An adult whose development was disrupted by adversity or trauma has a 'wobbly' developmental structure. She or he may have less resilience under stress and may react to stress by coping as if a child (regressing). We call this 'developmental collapse', or *regressing* to a developmental stage when the foundation was more solid (Pearson, 2013).

Attachment disorder and adult mental health

Children with disrupted development following adversity are often labelled as having 'attachment disorder'. This label is associated with lowered cognitive ability (IQ, concentration, attention, memory), high levels of anxiety, 'developmental collapse', lack of emotional and behavioural regulation, dysfunctional relationships and low self-esteem. Similar disturbances of functioning are seen in adults labelled with 'emotionally unstable personality disorder' (EUPD, also called BPD) and also in complex PTSD. These patterns are commonly seen in adults with a history of adversity in childhood. Adult complex PTSD includes problems with affect, impulse control, attention, consciousness (dissociation), self-perception, relationships and somatisation. It could be argued that the labels we use reflect the age of the individual, rather than a difference in presentation, and that complex PTSD and EUPD/BPD are adult expressions of attachment disorder.

CBT+ works to address all of these problems through a variety of strategies and skills teaching, which progress from stabilising the client and developing a trusting therapeutic relationship through tackling trauma and acquiring new skills for living.

References

American Psychiatric Association. (2013). *Diagnostic and Statistical Manual of Mental Disorders*, 5th Edition. Washington, DC: APA.

Felitti, V. J., Anda, R. F., Nordenberg, D., Williamson, D. F., Alison, B. et al. (1998). Relationship of childhood abuse to many of the leading causes of death in adults: The adverse childhood experiences (ACE) study. *American Journal of Preventive Medicine*, *14*(4), 245–258.

Kennedy, F. (2013). Dissociation, personality and psychopathology, a cognitive approach. In F. Kennedy, H. Kennerley, & D. Pearson (Eds.), *Cognitive Behavioural Approaches to the Understanding and Treatment of Dissociation*. London: Routledge.

Kessler, R. C., McLaughlin, K. A., Green, J. G., & Gruber, M. J. (2010). Child adversities and adult psychopathology in the WHO world mental health surveys. *British Journal of Psychiatry*, *197*(5), 378–385.

Kinderman, P., Schwannauer, M., Pontin, P., & Tai, S. (2013). Psychological processes mediate the impact of familial risk, social circumstances and life events on mental health. *PLoS One*, *8*(10), e76564.

Pearson, D. (2013). Can the foundations of dissociation be found in childhood? In F. Kennedy, H. Kennerley, & D. Pearson (Eds.), *Cognitive Behavioural Approaches to the Understanding and Treatment of Dissociation*. London: Routledge.

Read, J. & Bentall, R. (2010). Negative childhood experiences and mental health: Theoretical, clinical and primary implications. *British Journal of Psychiatry*, *200*, 89–91.

Seery, M. (2011). Resilience: A silver lining to experiencing adverse life events? *Current Directions in Psychological Science*, *20*(6), 390–394.

Van der Hart, O. & Steele, K. (2013). Structural dissociation of the personality. In F. Kennedy, H. Kennerley, & D. Pearson (Eds.), *Cognitive Behavioural Approaches to the Understanding and Treatment of Dissociation*, 206–220. London: Routledge.

12

Mindfulness theory

This chapter investigates the theoretical underpinnings of mindfulness as used in a Western context for mental health interventions. We briefly look at whether mindfulness works and then at theories as to how it might work. There is a growing body of research on mindfulness, including investigations into its effectiveness and the mechanisms through which it works. Two good sources for more information are Ruth Baer's and Rebecca Crane's books in this series.

Research on mindfulness

Systematic reviews by Gu et al. (2015) and van der Velden et al. (2015) provide reasonable evidence that mindfulness does work in terms of symptom reduction and other outcomes. For anxiety and depression, outcomes are generally comparable to drug treatment outcomes. Cancer-related pain, depression, anxiety, stress and quality of life were shown to be improved in a recent systematic review by Ngamkhan, Holden and Smith (2019). Mindfulness treatments reduce the frequency and severity of substance misuse, intensity of craving for psychoactive substances and severity of stress (Howard et al., 2017). For psychosis, Austin and Bradshaw's (2017) systematic review showed positive outcomes and no adverse effects of mindfulness interventions. Across the research, the types of mindfulness-based interventions studies vary, for example mindfulness-based stress reduction and mindfulness-based CBT, and include different methods of delivery (self-help, group, individual) and lengths of intervention. Also, less data are available on how sustainable gains are and how much continuous practice is needed to sustain the gains made.

Mediation studies show that mindfulness-based interventions produce increased mindfulness skills, which in turn produce improved mental health outcomes (Baer, 2019). Baer also reviewed the research on candidate processes involved in mindfulness effectiveness. She concluded that seven processes were the best candidates:

- Reduced cognitive reactivity. During mindfulness a negative mood activates fewer negative thought patterns
- Reduced emotional reactivity. We recover faster from unpleasant experiences
- Fewer repetitive negative thoughts. Rumination may decrease with mindfulness practice, or else our relationship with our ruminations may change (we may take them less seriously, be less engaged with or caught up in them)
- Increased self-compassion. We may become able to feel kindness in the face of suffering; to be aware of being part of larger human experience; to be able to hold our thoughts and feelings in balanced awareness
- Decentring. We experience a change in perspective: we view our thoughts as fleeting internal events rather than important signals for action
- Psychological flexibility. We can still act in a values-based way no matter how we feel at the time
- Increased positive affect. We experience more positive emotions and also notice the positive emotions available to us

Mindfulness-to-meaning

The mindfulness-to-meaning theory (MMT) (Garland et al., 2015) is a process model explaining how mindfulness might produce an upward spiral of positive psychological growth. MMT provides a theoretical framework for how mindfulness can create a virtuous cycle of appraisal→ decentring→ metacognitive awareness. In addition, mindfulness increases positive reappraisals, which then extend into broader contexts. The effect of this may be that conditioned negative emotional responses become extinguished. At the same time, positive affect and wellbeing are promoted.

Human beings are constantly filtering and selecting information from inside and outside the body. The challenge is how we regulate what information is attended to and what meanings we make from our experience. MMT proposes that mindfulness practice, over time, can lead to a deepened capacity for meaning-making. It develops a capacity to positively reappraise experiences of suffering. It also helps amplify the positive affect related to natural rewards through 'savouring'. These reappraisals and increased positive affect allow meaningful engagement with the world and other people, supporting individual growth and promoting wellbeing. All this transforms the nature of our personal narrative or 'autobiographical self'.

Over the course of mindfulness practice, attentional processes can become attuned towards positive information in the internal and external environment (Kiken & Shook, 2011). MMT hypothesises that attentional tuning towards positive stimuli, and reframing our relationship with negative stimuli, will generate more positive

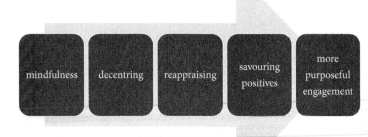

Figure 12.1 Mindfulness-to-meaning theory

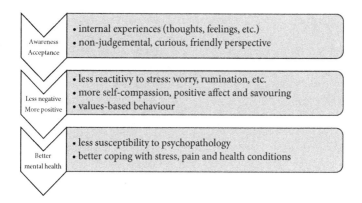

Figure 12.2 Simple mindfulness-to-meaning theory

affect. Cognitive reappraisal will simultaneously occur as part of the virtuous cycle, increasing wellbeing and moving us towards experiencing ourselves as part of the wider human community (pro-sociality). Figure 12.1 summarises these processes, while Figure 12.2 is a simpler version.

Summary

Mindfulness does work and it is effective for a variety of presentations. Potential ways in which it works include perspective-taking (decentring); increasing positive and decreasing negative emotions; increasing self-compassion; increasing flexible responding; and increasing cognitive and emotional regulation. A virtuous cycle of decentring, reappraising and savouring positives results in more meaningful engagement with the world and other people.

Suggested further reading

Baer, R. (2014). *Mindfulness-Based Treatment Approaches*, 2nd Edition. Cambridge, MA: Academic Press.

Crane, R. (2017). *Mindfulness-Based Cognitive Therapy: Distinctive Features (CBT Distinctive Features)*, 2nd Edition. London: Routledge.

References

Austin, J. & Bradshaw, T. (2017). Mindfulness interventions for psychosis: A systematic review of the literature. *Journal of Psychiatric and Mental Health Nursing*, 24(1), 69–83.

Baer, R. (2019). Assessment of mindfulness by self-report. *Current Opinion in Psychology*, 28, 42–48.

Garland, E. L., Farb, N. A., Philippe, R., Goldin, P. R., & Fredrickson, B. L. (2015). Mindfulness broadens awareness and builds eudaimonic meaning: A process model of mindful positive emotion regulation. *Psychological Inquiry*, 28(4), 293–314.

Gu, J., Strauss, C., Bond, R., & Cavanagh, K. (2015). How do mindfulness-based cognitive therapy and mindfulness-based stress reduction improve mental health and wellbeing? A systematic review and meta-analysis of mediation studies. *Clinical Psychology Review*, 37(1), 1–12.

Howard, M. O., Garland, E. L., McGovern, P., & Lazar, M. (2017). Mindfulness treatment for substance misuse: A systematic review and meta-analysis. *Journal of Substance Abuse Treatment*, 75, 62–69.

Kiken, L. G. & Shook, N. J. (2011). Looking-up: Mindfulness increases positive judgments and reduces negativity bias. *Social Psychological and Personality Science*, 2(4), 425–531.

Ngamkhan, S., Holden, J., & Smith, E. L. (2019). A systematic review: Mindfulness intervention for cancer-related pain. *Asia Journal of Oncology Nursing*, 6(2), 161–169.

van der Velden, A. M., Kuyken, W., Wattar, U., Crane, C., Pallesen, K. J. et al. (2015). A systematic review of mechanisms of change in mindfulness-based cognitive therapy in the treatment of recurrent major depressive disorder. *Clinical Psychology Review*, 37, 26–39.

13

Behavioural analysis

In this chapter we reflect on behavioural analysis and its relevance for clinicians, as well as the world of relational frame theory (RFT), since this is of fundamental relevance to ACT and can add greatly to our understanding of human language and behaviour. Analysis of our own behaviour as therapists means we remain alert to the contingencies operating in our interactions with the client.

Principles of behaviour analysis: operant conditioning

Operant conditioning describes the relationship between behaviour and the environment. Positive and negative reinforcement are the sources of the 'short-term gains' described in Chapter 25.

Positive reinforcement

At the risk of 'teaching granny to suck eggs', we would like to briefly revisit positive reinforcement. A reinforcer is *anything delivered contingent on a response that increases the likelihood that the response will occur again*. The consequence of an operant (an action or a behaviour or a 'response') is associated with ('contingent' upon) the action, so that the operant (behaviour) is strengthened. This could be an increase in frequency, duration or intensity of the behaviour. It is tempting to equate positive reinforcement with reward and with pleasurable sensation. However, the definition of reinforcement is circular: we only know if we have reinforcement if the behaviour is strengthened. Positive reinforcement is not always obviously pleasant: pain works as a positive reinforcer in some instances. What seems a positive consequence may not always be so, for example, individuals who have been praised during abuse may find praise aversive.

Negative reinforcement

Negative reinforcement also increases the strength of a behaviour. In this contingency, a behaviour results in *escape from* or *avoidance of* an aversive state or experience. This contingency governs most of our clients' lives, as, over time, their behaviour has become focused on avoiding pain. Behaviours such as self-harm, binge-eating, substance abuse, checking and rituals often serve the function of changing a person's internal aversive state into something less aversive. Clients may not be aware that this is happening, or they may be able to describe 'relief'. Avoidant behaviours are problematic, in that they shrink lives as they take over, denying us opportunities to learn new things, to grow and to experience joy.

Principles of behaviour analysis: classical conditioning

Human beings are born 'hard-wired' with built-in responses such as salivation, the startle response, sexual responses and attachment responses. These responses are 'elicited' by specific stimuli, for example, the sight or smell of food elicits salivation. Pavlov's work showed how hard-wired or 'unconditioned' responses could be manipulated by being paired with new stimuli that would not normally elicit them. We are all familiar with his work pairing a bell with food. This 'paired associated learning' is also vitally important in behaviour analysis. It is worth revisiting the terminology used in classical conditioning paradigms. The term for the eliciting stimulus (e.g. food) is 'unconditioned stimulus', when it is eliciting the hard-wired response (e.g. salivation). After the food has been paired with another, not hard-wired, stimulus (e.g. a bell), the new stimulus (the bell) becomes a 'conditioned stimulus'. When the conditioned stimulus (e.g. the bell) is presented it now elicits the same response (e.g. salivation) as the unconditioned stimulus. Note that the response (salivation) stays the same, but is renamed the 'conditioned response' if it occurs in response to the conditioned stimulus (the bell). In traumatic events, paired associate learning is very common. A client with health anxiety experienced upper back pain as well as feelings of dread, just prior to a heart attack (feelings of dread often occur prior to and during a heart attack). Following this paired associate learning (pairing upper back pain with feelings of dread), whenever he had upper back pain, he also had feelings of dread. Ruth's father had blue eyes, and she had panic attacks when she met other men with blue eyes, even though she was not initially aware of the connection.

Principles of behaviour analysis: relational frame theory

There is insufficient scope in this book to do justice to RFT and further reading is suggested below. RFT is a theory of verbal behaviour (human language) attributed to Steven Hayes and colleagues. It refers to our ability to 'derive' relationships ('relations') amongst things, and the words that represent them. It explains our ability to think and to learn very fast compared to animals. As human beings we do not need to have relations between things directly reinforced in order to learn about them. If we reinforce selecting X in the presence of Y, and also reinforce Z in the presence of Y, when we present Z, humans will select X and vice-versa, even though the 'relation' between Z and X has never been directly trained. This capacity allows for an exponential growth of our ability to derive relations during childhood, and our extraordinary capacity for thought and language. The take-away here is probably to remember that for human beings, behaviour does not need to be classically or operantly conditioned, although these processes are just as vital to our learning as they are in animals. We can include derived relations in our formulations of behaviour.

Contingency management

In addition to using behavioural theory to analyse behaviour, we use it to change behaviour. This includes positive reinforcement of desired (adaptive, effective, skilled) behaviour. The best reinforcers are as similar to 'natural' reinforcers as possible, for example, a smile when a client reports doing homework. Reinforcers should be delivered as soon after a response as possible. The minimum effective reinforcer should be used. Negative reinforcement can also be used to strengthen a behaviour, as when a client completes homework in order to avoid disappointing us. Punishment is an operant contingency used to *reduce* undesired (target) behaviours. Mild therapist disappointment or disapproval, or a comment on how we have missed a chance to progress, are often powerful 'punishers' in terms of reducing behaviour, and should be used cautiously. In RFT terms, we can change derived relations by providing the client with opportunities to learn new things using exposure, behavioural experiments, metaphors, increasing willingness and other ACT techniques.

Summary

Analysis of the functions of behaviours not only informs our shared understanding with the client in CBT+, but also helps us to reduce target behaviours and increase skills. We aim to manipulate the contingencies as best we can to keep both therapist and client on track.

Suggested further reading

Hayes, S. C. (2004). Acceptance and commitment therapy, relational frame theory, and the third wave of behavioural and cognitive therapies. *Behavior Therapy*, *35*, 639–665.

14

Re-living and re-scripting

In Chapter 11 we explored why childhood trauma and neglect are important in the development of psychological problems, and in Chapter 27 'Tackling trauma' we will give an overview of how to approach re-living and re-scripting practically in CBT+. This chapter aims to lay the groundwork by thinking about how re-living and re-scripting interventions work, and what the indications might be for choosing between them.

How re-living and re-scripting work

The debate about how re-living and re-scripting work is ongoing. Both re-living and re-scripting are special forms of exposure work for trauma, where the client is invited to re-visit the trauma in imagination, as vividly as possible. In the first case, the client re-lives the trauma, speaking in the first person and present tense. In the second case, the therapist helps the client to 'change the script' of the trauma so that the client ends up in a safe place and experiences self-compassion.

The most accepted behavioural explanation of why exposure works is the habituation model, that is, repeatedly experiencing a previously avoided stimulus leads to a reduction in responsiveness to it. Foa's (2011) protocol for treating PTSD reflects this model. A cognitive behavioural approach adds cognitive restructuring to behavioural exposure, helping the client to change the meaning of the experience. Ehlers and Clark's (2000) protocol for PTSD reflects this model. An ACT approach emphasises how exposure, or 'sitting with' or 'making room for' avoided emotions and experiences, can lead to new derived relations, allowing discrimination between 'I, here, now' and 'Me, there, then'. A CFT approach develops the compassionate mind and uses self–self and self–other compassion to change the meaning of the experience and reduce emotions like shame and blame. Schema therapy (not one of our four therapies mentioned in CBT+) is also strong on therapist-guided re-scripting, with the therapist entering the traumatic situation in imagination to change the script initially, later handing over responsibility to the client.

Most of these approaches require a change in the meaning of the experience to work. Trauma is frequently involved not just in PTSD but also in a great number of presentations, such as psychosis, generalised anxiety, obsessive compulsive disorder (OCD), depression, bipolar disorder, panic disorder, social anxiety, eating disorders, BPD and DID. Trauma and neglect may show up as direct intrusions from the past, or as thematically related beliefs, feelings, images, voices, body sensations, fears and nightmares.

Pros and cons of re-living and re-scripting

Re-living approaches have a solid evidence base for their effectiveness, but a higher drop-out rate than re-scripting approaches, especially when used with highly fearful or avoidant clients. Re-scripting approaches have a growing evidence base and allow client and therapist a gentler way to approach trauma. Some traumas are really too horrific even for therapists to endure: a refugee forced to kill her own child benefited from a re-scripting where she was able to bury him according to the proper tribal rituals, rather than the therapist asking her to re-live the experience.

Arguments for choosing re-scripting

We have found re-scripting more willingly accepted by clients and more effective in changing the meaning of past trauma. Hardy (2017) argues that when trauma appears as thematically related to the client's symptoms, rather than as a direct intrusion, re-scripting may be more effective. For example, a person with paranoia may have a history of severe bullying and personal attacks. Hearing voices that are shaming and humiliating towards him could be a thematically related result of his past. Re-scripting the bullying, with the therapist protecting him and reassuring him in imagination, allows the client to experience comfort and safety, rather than simply a reduction in fear. Since new learning is at the core of CBT+, it seems to us that this approach offers a richer transformation for the client and helps get needs met faster.

Building trust and waiting: an alternative approach

We would like to finish by mentioning an alternative approach, especially useful when amnesia for trauma is present. Tell-tale signs of this are not only when the client has very little recall of their past, but also when there is a globalised cheerful response of 'everything was fine'. Just by building trust, developing attachment and staying alongside a client, we often see the 'repair work' happen. Amnesia begins to dissipate and with it, new material emerges, which allows new meanings to be made. The client may realise her family has not been the safe place it should have been. There can be devastating consequences and the client may move back and forth between old and new ways of perceiving. Growing up in an abusive world, a child usually perceives family as normal. This assumption stays until adulthood and often requires the therapist to name it as abuse. We have found sitting alongside the client to be very effective. Re-living and re-scripting can be used alongside this approach, if appropriate.

Suggested further reading

Stopa, L. (2009). *Imagery and the Threatened Self: Perspectives on Mental Imagery and the Self in Cognitive Therapy*. London: Routledge.

References

Ehlers, A. & Clark, D. M. (2000). A cognitive model of posttraumatic stress disorder. *Behaviour Research and Therapy*, *38*, 319–345.

Foa, E. B. (2011). Prolonged exposure therapy: Past, present, and future. *Depression and Anxiety*, *28*(12), 1043–1047.

Hardy, A. (2017). Pathways from trauma to psychotic experiences: A theoretically informed model of posttraumatic stress in psychosis. *Frontiers in Psychology*, *8*(697), 1–20.

15

Dealing with dissociation

Dissociation is much more common than generally thought (Lowenstein, 2018). It is often a consequence of trauma, especially when the victim has been helpless, and is a mediator between trauma and mental health problems. If not identified and addressed in therapy, progress may be impossible as the client is neither 'present' nor processing information. We start with a definition of dissociation, describe how it affects functioning and discuss treatment in a CBT+ context.

What is dissociation?

In 1889, Pierre Janet described dissociation as a failure to integrate experiences (memories, perceptions, etc.) that are normally associated. Symptoms such as amnesia, depersonalisation, derealisation and identity confusion result from 'emergency' biological responses. Dissociation is the opposite of mindfulness, as it serves to reduce present moment awareness. It is a very physical reaction to very high levels of threat, involving the amygdala and other brain and body structures in shutting down, freezing and fainting responses. Survival-wise, dissociation is useful when escape is impossible, for example, when a mouse is cornered by a cat, being still and unresponsive is best. But in humans these responses can persist, being triggered whenever there are stimuli present that are similar to aspects of the previous trauma.

How does dissociation affect functioning?

Dissociation as a set of shutting down responses can affect many aspects of functioning. Broad categories are memory, perception/ consciousness, somatic/bodily experience and sense of self.

Memory

Clients may have amnesia for past events (e.g. a childhood trauma); for the recent past (e.g. yesterday's therapy session); for important personal information (e.g. one's own address). Amnesia is also seen in 'losing time' or fugue states, where the person lives for a time in another state of consciousness or self-state, then 'comes to' having lost the time spent in the other state.

Perception

Perception can be disturbed by hallucinations, flashbacks and nightmares. All of these can be construed as intrusions into awareness of aspects of past traumatic events thematically directly or thematically related to past trauma (dissociation is not the only route to these experiences). Consciousness is affected by 'spacing out', detachment, losing time, trance-like states, out of body experiences and inability to think.

Somatic experience

Dissociation can produce non-organic pain, non-epileptic seizures, somatic re-experiencing, and lowered body temperature and heart rate.

Sense of self

Dissociation can affect development of identity – chronic trauma in childhood can lead to the development of dissociated self-states. The individual affected will have reduced levels of awareness, acceptance and control of their self-states. Identity disturbance can be seen in BPD and DID as well as in other disorders.

Dissociation is present in many disorders, not only those classified as dissociative. It is found in anxiety disorders such as OCD and panic disorder, in eating disorders and in psychosis.

A model of dissociation

In our CBT model of dissociation (Kennedy et al., 2004) we describe three 'levels' of information processing that dissociation can affect:

- Perception
- Experience
- Personality

This is a transdiagnostic model consistent with the transdiagnostic approach of CBT+. The Wessex Dissociation Scale (Kennedy et al., 2004) was designed to be used by clinicians to assess the extent of dissociation across the three levels.

How can we treat dissociation?

The skills used in CBT+ can be very helpful for treating dissociation, especially mindful observing and describing skills. Using the three levels model to formulate the effects of dissociation is also helpful.

Level 1

Level 1 dissociation is when information processing shuts down in the early stages. In the therapy room this looks like 'spacing out': the client glazes over and is no longer 'present'. More extreme presentations can involve loss of consciousness. Observing and describing the triggers for this and bringing them to the awareness of client and therapist is a good place to start. The opposite Level 1 presentation involves intrusions into perception such as hallucinations, nightmares and images. These are seen as the effects of dissociation being incomplete and allowing 'leakage' into awareness. Grounding work is a central technique: a simple and easy 'noticing' ritual should be over-practised when the client is not dissociating. For example, the client should ask and answer: 'What colour is my top? What colour is the floor? What is my name?' Therapist and client should agree a 'starting signal' such as a handclap: at first the therapist will prompt the client to use the noticing ritual, starting with a handclap, later handing over to the client as awareness of triggers is built. Intrusions can be re-scripted, as described in Chapter 27, making a preferred image and 'anchoring' that image to pressure on the hand (e.g. thumb on the palm, pressure on the back of the hand). Practice is central to success.

Level 2

The person's 'Wheel of Experience' is affected. Thoughts, feelings, body sensations and behaviours can each or all be shut down. The person may become unable to think or to feel fear, to carry out some action or to connect to their body. CBT+ interventions include inviting the client to imagine what it would be like if she or he could experience the dissociated sensations, feelings or thoughts. Cheerleading and confidence that it is possible for these things to change is vital. The opposite presentation is intrusions of thoughts, feelings, body sensations and behaviours. It is useful to provide an understanding of the origins of these for the client and stay calm and confident that they will change.

Level 3

The extent to which identity is affected can be assessed by observing and describing whether the client has dissociated (unintegrated) self-states. These may be aspects of the self that are outside the client's awareness. The therapist may observe the client behaving very differently in or between sessions and there may be evidence of amnesia, not remembering what was said or done in one self-state when the client is in another self-state. In extreme cases, the client may not perceive other self-states as 'me' but see them as 'other', a characteristic of DID. In less extreme cases, the client may have awareness of self-states but be unable to control or choose which self-state to be in, and have little acceptance of or an active dislike for herself in some self-states. When dissociation affects the self in this way, it is important to 'map the system', that is, to mindfully observe and describe all self-states, using the client's own awareness as well as observations and information from others. The next step is to clarify values the client can endorse in every self-state and work towards therapy goals. The aim is to have a functioning 'team' of self-states, rather than a client at war with herself.

Suggested further reading

Kennedy, F. C., Kennerley, H., & Pearson, D. (Eds.). (2013) *Cognitive Behavioural Approaches to the Understanding and Treatment of Dissociation*. London: Routledge.

References

Kennedy, F., Clarke, S., Stopa, L., Bell, L., Rouse, H., Ainsworth, C. et al. (2004). Towards a cognitive model and measure of dissociation. *Journal of Behavior Therapy and Experimental Psychiatry*, *35*(1), 25–48.

Lowenstein, R. J. (2018). Dissociation debates: Everything you know is wrong. *Dialogues in Clinical Neuroscience*, *20*(3), 229–242.

THE DISTINCTIVE PRACTICAL FEATURES OF CBT+

16

Complex case: Ruth

Now that we have discussed the theoretical aspects of CBT+, we move on to the distinctive practical features of CBT+. Most of Part II uses the acronym NAVIGATES as a means to help therapists remember what to do in a practical way. To get us started, in this and the next chapter Ruth and Stuart, both with complex problems, are introduced and we follow them through therapy in the following chapters. Ruth is a woman who has a life based around avoidance. Recognising this avoidance of anxiety and painful thoughts is essential for the therapist to notice. Ruth's problems are long term and reflect damage that started when she was abused as a young child.

Ruth

In the supermarket about mid-morning, Ruth put a bottle of vodka in her basket and one in her coat pocket. As she did this, walking towards the checkout, she was anxious, her legs were shaking and she was sweating. Ruth had been caught shoplifting before, but had got away with it many times. As she walked home along the high street, she had no recollection of being in the supermarket and seemed to be on 'automatic pilot'. Back in her flat, she drank most of a bottle of vodka and thought about her life. She started crying and then fell asleep until early evening. This was her normal daily routine when not an inpatient at the local mental health unit.

Ruth is now in her forties, but life started going wrong when she was about six years old. Memories come and go, but she remembers that there was something wrong with her mum. Mum stopped looking after the house and her daughter, stopped cooking, doing the washing, shopping and later stopped getting out of bed altogether. There were many arguments and she remembers hearing bangs and her mum screaming and crying. For about four years her dad would come into her bedroom during the night and get into her bed. It is not possible for Ruth to remember what happened during these times. When she tries to think about them she feels stabbing pains 'down below' and vomits. This was the time when life started going wrong and somehow it just never stopped.

Ruth tried to tell her mum that she did not like Dad coming into her room. Mum looked blank and shook her head. She told Ruth not to lie, that she had ruined everything and was a 'nasty piece of stuff'. School also started going badly, Ruth could not concentrate and other children were calling her 'smelly' and 'scruffy'. During lessons Ruth started 'disappearing': feeling that she was floating and not part of the lesson or indeed at school. She learnt little and had no friends. Her teacher was worried and asked her if she was ill. Ruth said that she did not like her dad. Miss Smith said that all parents loved their children and not to worry. Ruth left school without any qualifications and started working at a café for cash.

The café job lasted for about a year until Ruth tried to kill herself by taking pills and vodka. She was admitted to a mental health unit where she found the staff much more supportive and caring than her parents. At 42 years old Ruth had been admitted to that unit about 20 times and was known by the staff as a regular. Often Ruth could not remember why she was admitted or any of the events around that time. She thought the admissions were often connected to relationships going wrong. Nearly all her relationships started off supportively but ended up abusive, leaving her feeling unlovable, worthless, dirty and often injured. These beliefs about herself were confirmed by voices she heard, which sounded a bit like Mum telling her that she was unlovable and dirty. Ruth could not stop the voices, which made her feel angry, sad and excited all at the same time. They would last for about three hours or until she drank a bottle of vodka and sometimes took about half a bottle of prescription (pain-killer) tablets.

During her admissions Ruth had been told that she has border-line personality disorder, depression and anxiety. One psychiatrist said she thought Ruth might have psychosis. Lots of pills have been prescribed over the years, but one thing that Ruth had learnt is that cutting her arms and drinking a bottle of vodka works faster. Sadly, she had also learnt that when she wakes up, she feels much, much worse.

17

Complex case: Stuart

In Chapter 16 we were introduced to Ruth. When her therapist talked about her life, Ruth described problems that started at six years of age and continued to get more complex during her childhood and then her adult life. These problems were developmental, psychological and possibly organic. This sort of long history is not always the case. Stuart was a bus driver, happily married with two children. He described his childhood as happy, mum worked in the super-market and Dad was an engineer at the washing machine factory. Stuart had friends at school, was not academic but really loved cars and lorries. He became a bus driver, married Ellie, who was one of the best looking girls in the class when they were at school, and bought a house on the new estate. Stuart had never known adversity, he was proud of his wife, family, house, job and children. Not everybody realised how much skill is needed to drive a bus around the city and just how good it makes you feel, not being an ordinary driver. And yet, in a matter of a few seconds an event happened that changed all of this.

It was three years ago and Stuart was driving the family car, with his two children aged four and six in their car seats in the back. He was talking to Ellie, his wife, on his hands-free, sorting out what he needed to get from the supermarket after dropping the children off at their grandparents. Although Stuart cannot remember exactly what happened, a lorry hit their car broadside as they went round a roundabout. Stuart hit his head on the door pillar; he was concussed but did not lose consciousness. Stuart remembered seeing Tom his six-year-old son with a cut on his forehead, which was bleeding. Janie, Stuart's four-year-old daughter, looked lifeless, just sitting in her car seat not moving. Although it is difficult to describe, Stuart recalled that as he looked at his children it was as though they were a distance away and not in his car at all. Stuart felt frozen and unable to move – he thought his children were dead. Very quickly the police and ambulance arrived, the children were taken to hospital and Stuart was taken to hospital in another ambulance. At the hospital Stuart was told that both his children were OK and not seriously injured. By the time that Stuart was walking about feeling able to manage, Ellie had arrived and was with the children.

Now, three years after the accident, Stuart was still off work and attending a local mental health unit as an out-patient. He had flash-backs of the accident, which felt so real he almost believed that he was back in the accident, seeing his children in their car seats dead. Flash-backs tended to happen in the evenings when Stuart was with the children before they went to bed. If Stuart tried to drive the family car he experienced high levels of anxiety that made him feel sick, with a fast heart-beat, sweating and feelings of panic. Life had really changed for Stuart, he felt useless as a parent and unable or unsafe to care for the children. After the accident Stuart was unable to stop thinking that he was not able to protect or help his children at the time of the accident. He just remembered being 'paralysed' and seeing his children as though they were a distance away.

Not only did Stuart feel that he was no longer able to be an effective parent, he also believed he was an ineffective husband. Stuart could not continue with his job as a bus driver and eventually lost his job altogether. This caused financial problems and his relationship with Ellie was extremely stressed. After Stuart lost his job he started drinking at lunch time instead of eating. Stuart drank more than half a bottle of whiskey a day, which made him feel better but was increasing the family's financial problems. Stuart was hoping that the therapist at the local unit would be able stop these awful flash-backs, feelings of panic and uselessness, but he really had no idea how.

Stuart's therapist recognised that due to a traumatic event his ability to follow his values had been destroyed. Stuart valued being the man of the house, a husband and dad who could provide for and protect his family. He had a proper job that needed his skills. Stuart would say that this was how his dad was and that this provided his role model. After the crash Stuart was no longer able to live the life that he valued. He saw himself as an ineffective husband, dad and man. He was drinking to avoid the pain that his thoughts caused, but this short-term gain was just piling on the long-term pain.

18

Mindfulness for clients

We would like to emphasise the central role of mindfulness in CBT+ and the importance of this skill for clients and for therapists. This chapter shows how to orient the client to mindfulness and why it is important. It describes the 'mindfulness journey' that takes the client from easy to more challenging practices. We also discuss the need for skills generalisation so that mindfulness becomes embedded into the client's way of life.

What is mindfulness and why is it important? Orienting the client

A major challenge is that it is often not immediately obvious to clients how mindfulness can help. Mindfulness is the dialectical opposite of avoidance, involving willing acceptance of direct experience. If we explain this to clients, the question will be 'But why?' We often need to overcome considerable reluctance to experience aversive feelings, memories, etc. We also need to change how the client relates to their internal world, learning to 'make room' for unpleasant events and sensations. From ACT we see how language allows us to 'time travel' into the past and into the future, where rumination and anxiety may take over. Here is an explanation we use, from *Get Your Life Back: The Most Effective Therapies for a Better You:*

> Mindfulness is focusing on the present moment with awareness and acceptance, without judging. Because of language, humans are very good at 'time travel', spending a lot of time visiting the past, with thoughts like:

'If only …'
'I wish …'
'That was a bad thing s/he/I did'

These are 'ruminations', at the centre of low mood and depression. There may also be images of the events. Our minds also visit the future, imagining the worst:

'What if …'

These thoughts and images are usually connected with anxiety.

We make judgements about things being bad or good, compare ourselves to others and catastrophise. So we miss what is around right now. Life can slip by and we can miss it. This is where mindfulness comes in.

Mindfulness is:

- Mindfulness is like taking your mind to the gym
- Mindfulness is about 'sitting with' feelings not changing them
- Mindfulness is about doing things with awareness, not 'on automatic pilot'
- Mindfulness is being non-judgemental. We use the example of a woman who decided to suspend her judgements, which made her always choose egg for her lunch sandwich. She found she enjoyed ham, too!

Mindfulness is not:

- Relaxation
- Feeling better
- Pushing away thoughts (they always come back)
- Emptying your mind (there's always something going on in there)

Sometimes when we practice mindfulness we will feel relaxed. Other times we will feel restless. Sometimes it will be easy. Other times it will be hard. We are working to accept whatever it is, however it is at the time.

After this introduction we are ready to start doing some mindfulness, rather than just talking about it.

The mindfulness journey

To take the client on a mindfulness journey, we recommend starting with easily accessible, relatively pleasant, external foci, before moving onto internal experiences such as internal experiences and breath, and then onto thoughts and feelings. The aim is to take the client to a level of skill that makes them able to stay mindful in even the most challenging contexts. There are some exercises to guide this journey in the next chapter. They are also available as recordings from the website www.getyourlifeback.global. The client should be enabled to move from easy to difficult; outside to inside focus; concrete to abstract; pleasant to painful. It is also important to set some open, observing-what-is-there exercises, as well as exercises with a specific focus. The journey has to be modified and adapted for the individual client. For example, an anxious client will often struggle with mindfulness of breath because she or he will be in the habit of monitoring for changes in breath signalling anxiety or panic.

Skills practice and generalisation

Since mindfulness is a skill to be learned, therapists need to consider the need for skills generalisation. We can facilitate this in various ways:

- Mindfulness skills need to be practised in every possible context, sitting, standing, walking, eyes closed/open, with/without a bell, etc.
- As skills increase, we can expose the client to more and more challenging situations in which to practice: initially the client

may practice mindfully chatting with a neighbour, later tackling difficult conversations or public speaking, for example

- 'Instant' practices such as 'Where are my feet? Where is my breath?' or 'one breath in and one out' allow access to mindfulness quickly and when needed
- Reframing global negative judgements: inviting the client to observe and describe, for example, when the client says 'I'm useless', teach him/her to reframe as 'I'm having the thought "I'm useless"' and 'I'm feeling disgust'
- Beginning and ending each therapy session with mindfulness practice
- Taking a break during the session for mindfulness practice
- Asking the client what she or he would say about a situation from her 'wise (mindful) mind'
- Compassionate mindfulness work to develop self-acceptance (see Chapter 26)

Developing a 'mindful stance' that is an approach to life from a mindful awareness perspective, is the ultimate aim. We suggest that CBT+ sessions start and end with two-minute mindfulness practices and include role plays of mindful approaches to difficult situations as well as mindfulness homework assignments. The aim is for the client to use the skills learned in the formal practices spontaneously and whenever they are needed in everyday life.

Suggested further reading

Kennedy, F. & Pearson, D. (2017). *Get Your Life Back: The Most Effective Therapies for a Better You*. London: Constable.

Dunkley, C. & Stanton, M. (2016). *Teaching Clients to Use Mindfulness Skills: A Practical Guide*. London: Routledge.

19

Mindfulness exercises

Mindfulness 1: Get off automatic invites the client to notice how mindlessly we usually live and to try out doing something with full present moment awareness.

Think of something you usually do automatically, without thinking, maybe driving, eating, showering, drinking coffee, etc.

This means you will:

- Notice it
- Notice judgements, let them be there and bring your mind back to the task
- Do it with care
- Do not do anything else at the same time

Your thoughts will run off somewhere like untrained puppies in Figure 19.1, they are always wandering off and getting distracted.

This is expected, notice they have wandered, make a choice to leave the thoughts be and bring your mind back to the sensations, this needs practice.

Mindfulness 2: Eat a raisin has the external focus on a food object and provides a lot of sensory stimulation to be noticed mindfully 'turning the mind' repeatedly from distractions and back towards the desired focus.

With a raisin or similar, sit down with this food object in the palm of your hand:

LOOK: Take a close, mindful look at the object. Check out the colours, textures, shadows. Turn it over and look at the other side
SMELL: Hold the object below your nose – what do you smell?

Figure 19.1 Untrained thought puppies

© Liane Payne, reused from *Get Your Life Back: The Most Effective Therapies For A Better You* (2017) with permission

LISTEN: Take the object to your ear. Rub, squeeze and listen

TASTE: Put the object in your mouth, resting on your tongue. Notice your mouth salivating. Now move the object around your mouth a little, maybe pressing it against the roof of your mouth. Next slowly bite the object, and bite again. Notice changes in taste and texture. Then chew and swallow until most of the object has gone. Notice what remains after the object has gone

EXPAND: Let your awareness expand from the inside of your mouth to your whole body, then the whole room and the world around you. Keep this present moment awareness

Mindfulness 3: Breath is often a starting point for mindfulness practice, but those with panic or health anxiety, chronic obstructive pulmonary disease (COPD), heart problems, etc., may find it challenging and a more advanced practice.

Set a timer for five minutes

Sit down, straight back and neck

Close or half close your eyes, or focus on a point on the floor

Bring the spotlight of your attention to your breath, don't try to change it

Notice:

AIR IN: notice the air travelling over your upper lip and in through your nostrils. Perhaps it is cool as it comes in and warm as it comes out. Notice how your chest and tummy rise as your lungs fill and your ribcage expands. Is there a little pause at the top of the breath, or maybe a smooth transition to breathing out?

AIR OUT: observe the shrinking of the tummy and ribs and leaving the nostrils. Do not change your breath. Just observe it

The untrained puppy thoughts may arrive again with judgements – am I doing it right, will it help? Distractions may be an ache in your back or a tickle in your throat. You can 'fix' them by moving or coughing, or decide to resist the urges and see what happens. In either case, make the decision with awareness. Remember it is normal to get distracted. When you notice you have left your breath, be kind to yourself and gently bring your mind back to the breath. When the alarm goes off, bring your mind back to the room, keeping the present moment awareness of yourself and the world around you.

Mindfulness 4: Mindful stretch can generate self-critical judgements about body shape, not being fit enough, etc. It is a good opportunity to begin noticing these judgements and then turning the mind back to the sensations of the stretch.

Stand up. Lift your arms high above your head feeling the stretch throughout the arms, trying to touch the ceiling, let your head fall back and stand on tiptoes, feel this through your whole body

Next, plant your feet on the floor firmly, bend your knees a little and fold your upper body forward from the hips as far as you comfortably can. Just dangle there. Shake your head gently and let your arms flop forward. Notice your muscles, feel any discomfort, pleasure, warmth or stiffness, etc.

Uncurl slowly back to standing upright

Put your hands in the small of your back, push your hips forwards and lean back from the hips, squeezing your shoulder blades together, like being worn out after gardening

Straighten up

Put your hands on your hips and lean to the right, notice the muscles down the opposite side of your body – then to the left

Straighten up and shake out each arm and each leg

Notice the whole of your body

Now notice three things about the room or environment around you

Do all this with as much awareness and acceptance as you can manage today

Mindfulness 5: Thought soldiers teaches how to observe thoughts, giving them to imaginary marching soldiers (or ladybirds). Handing thoughts over rather than engaging with them is a great way to teach a different relationship with internal events.

> With a five-minute timer, sit (or stand) with your back and neck straight and your feet on the floor
>
> Imagine a row of soldiers or ladybirds marching through your head. Picture them if you can. If you cannot, just describe them in words
>
> Imagine them marching through your head, out of your ear, down your arm, across your lap, then up the other arm, back into your ear
>
> Notice your thoughts and give each one to a soldier. When you notice another thought, give it to another soldier, and so on (see Figure 19.2)

When your mind wanders, notice you have stopped doing this, gently bring your mind back to the task.

Mindfulness 6: Feelings helps us to gain a new perspective on emotional and physical pain by simply observing and describing it. Locate the pain within the body, then use your hands to 'take the pain out' of the body, hold it and describe it (colour, weight, shape, etc.). Welcome the pain back into the body teaching an acceptance stance (known in ACT as the 'physicalising exercise').

> Sit (or stand) with your back and neck straight and your feet on the floor
>
> Bring to mind an emotion, or pain in your body. Ask where in my body do I feel this pain or painful emotion? Take both of your hands and place them on that part of your body. Then (really do this) use your hands to take the pain out of your body and hold it in your hands in front of you, then:
>
> > LOOK: what is its colour, shape, size, is it see through, opaque, still or moving, solid, liquid, gas, etc.?
> >
> > FEEL: how heavy is it, what texture (rough, smooth, prickly) is it, is it sticky, hairy, maybe warm or cold?

Figure 19.2 Thought soldiers

© Liane Payne, reused from *Get Your Life Back: The Most Effective Therapies For A Better You* (2017) with permission

LISTEN: is it silent or does it make a noise?
SMELL: does it smell?

Place it back inside your body
Take a breath
Then again, take it back out. Check out what it looks, feels, sounds and smells like. Has it changed or is it just the same?
When you have finished observing and describing the pain, place it back into your body and leave it there

Mindfulness 7: Grounding re-centres the person back into the present moment, even in extreme circumstances where she or he may have lost contact with reality. We suggest a very simple routine, linked to a specific 'signal', which can be over-practised when the client is not in extremis, and used when they are. The signal and routine, together with a 'reminder', can be used by therapists or clients to bring the client back from distress, worrying about the past or future, confusion or dissociated states of mind:

> A reminder can be a lavender roll-on, an elastic band flick on wrist, stress ball squeeze, hold a hanky, tap the back of hand, etc.
> Ask and answer:

- What is the time and date?
- What is your name?
- What colour is the carpet or floor covering?

This needs to be practiced often when not spacing out or ruminating. To 'ground' quickly, just use the reminder instead of the three questions.

Mindfulness exercises are downloadable free from www.getyourlifeback.global

20

Motivation and commitment

Problems of motivation and commitment are often a great challenge to therapists, and can lead into the trap of persuading, cajoling and generally working harder than the client! If we do this, the client's natural reaction is to resist, withdraw and panic about letting us down, or to get angry with us for cornering her. This chapter introduces ways to deal with commitment at the outset and throughout therapy.

Obstacles to change

Many of us have personal learning histories, including failing to meet our own or others' goals; being betrayed, abandoned and let down; being abused and taken advantage of; being taught that we are worthless; and disappointing others and letting them down. From the various horrible positions such histories leave us in, it is very understandable that we would have problems agreeing to take on the difficult task of changing ourselves, even with the help of a therapist. Consciously or unconsciously avoiding commitment means sparing ourselves the horrible feelings that anticipating disaster brings.

The DBT see-saw of acceptance and change

A major metaphor from DBT is the see-saw. On opposite ends of the see-saw balance are acceptance and change, meaning we constantly ask for change whilst surrounding the client with acceptance:

'You're perfect just as you are ... and you really need to change!' This approach allows the therapist to join with the client where she is without forcing things, at the same time as pushing for progress.

Validation

Used in all therapies, validation is key to making the client feel heard and valued. DBT offers six levels of validation:

- Look, listen, don't judge
- Reflect back what the client has said, check you have it correct
- Guess the feelings, thoughts, body sensations and behaviours/ urges the client may be having/have had (rather than ask 'How do you feel?', which the client may not be able to answer)
- Normalise the feelings, thoughts, etc. in light of the client's past learning
- Normalise the feelings, thoughts, etc. in light of the client's current context
- Radical genuineness; your honest response to the client

Be prepared to walk away

When we negotiate or bargain it is always important to be able to walk away and that the other person knows we are prepared to do so. Otherwise all the wiggle room lies with the other person. So, it is very powerful to approach the beginning sessions of therapy with a discussion, not of *what* you will work on, but of *whether* you will work at all:

- 'Is it the right time for you?'
- 'Am I the right therapist for you?'
- 'Are you committed enough?'
- 'What might go wrong between us?'

Commitment period

We find in supervision that many therapists insist they have indeed had the discussion above, but when they look back realise that the client had not fully understood or responded. We recommend really labouring this point, especially with clients with a history of not making it through another therapy. Commitment work is like building the foundation of a house, it needs to be solid to survive future bad weather. We recommend having a 'commitment period' in CBT+, as in DBT, during which either party is explicitly free to walk away. Then comes a contract, preferably signed, specifying how many sessions, how frequent, need for homework, what happens if sessions are missed and what behaviours will be worked on. Therapists interested in developing this further should study Linehan's (1993) work or Michaela Swales and Heidi Heard's (2016) book in this series.

Creative hopelessness

An ACT approach to commitment involves creative hopelessness. Here, the therapist listens carefully to all of the things the client has already tried, reflecting back empathetically. Once the list of efforts seems thoroughly exhausted, the therapist sums up by saying

> So, you have tried A and B and C (examples of what's been tried) which lead to X and Y and Z (various consequences but no change). Given that you have made all these efforts and still they haven't worked, would you be willing to try something new?

Compassion: it's not your fault

CFT also comes from a very validating and nurturing place at the outset of therapy. The explanation of 'it's not your fault' can be adapted to the client's own circumstances. It will involve an explanation of evolutionary theory so that it is clear that we are all evolved to expect the worst, look out for danger, compare our-selves with others and give up in the face of overwhelming odds or unpredictable outcomes. We explain that all of this is good for survival, however, for humans it can run out of control and cause suffering. ACT has a similar script about language, pointing out that as far as we know, humans are the only beings that can 'time travel': because we have words, we can ruminate about the past and anticipate future disaster in a way that animals cannot. The message is: 'It's not your fault, it's natural to be this way ... and you need to change'.

Clarifying values and goals throughout therapy

Every therapist knows it is important have goals, not just about reducing suffering but also about thriving: what makes an individ-ual's life worth living? CBT+ puts a great emphasis on thriving. As reflected in the following chapters, we are interested in reducing distress but also in living well. Clarifying values (see Chapter 23) is an opportunity to help the client identify what *kind of person* they want to be. Within this framework, we can set goals (see Chapter 25) to help them take baby steps and then bigger steps, away from their problems and towards being that person.

Commitment strategies

DBT offers a variety of 'commitment strategies' derived from moti-vational interviewing and from sales techniques. We love them. One of the best is 'pros and cons', where we simply sit with the client and go through all the advantages of, or reasons for, doing therapy, and the difficulties expected. No persuasion is needed from the therapist, just validation and information if there are misunder-standings. The difficulties are accepted and validated if they cannot be solved, and the client needs to decide whether to go ahead in the face of these difficulties.

Revisiting commitment

Although commitment work is vital at the outset of therapy, there will be ups and downs throughout the work and it will be necessary to stop, step back and revisit commitment work whenever necessary (when the client seems to be losing motivation). It is vital to keep the energy coming from the client as well as from the therapist.

Summary

Before starting on therapy, in CBT+ we recommend having several commitment, pre-therapy sessions, using commitment strategies and building self-compassion and willingness. This has the effect of increasing the client's motivation and the chances of success. Target behaviours are identified whilst both parties stay in the space of considering whether or not to go ahead with therapy. To learn more about target behaviours, please read the next chapter.

References

Linehan, M. M. (1993). *Cognitive Behaviour Therapy for Personality Disorders*. New York: Guilford Press.

Swales, M. A. & Heard, H. L. (2016). *Dialectical Behaviour Therapy (The CBT Distinctive Features Series)*. London: Routledge.

21

Name the problem behaviours

NAVIGATES

On first meeting a client, the therapist has a few options. The therapist needs accurate and detailed collection of information and thorough assessment. Alternatively, putting ourselves into the client's shoes, there is a need to be heard, understood and given hope. Hopelessness and shame are particularly difficult in therapeutic encounters, as they limit disclosure and block progress.

We call this aspect of CBT+ 'name the problem behaviours', because we think it is important to do some shame-busting and also to get clear with the client what the business of therapy is going to be. We can use an 'irreverent style' from DBT, going where angels fear to tread. But we should always balance this with mindful compassion, acceptance and a willingness to experience the client's own reality. This reality is usually only one perspective on the wider context in which the problem behaviours occur. It is the client's own story and whilst taking it very seriously, we need to hold it lightly.

Identifying target or problem behaviours is an essential part of CBT+ and is part of the commitment phase of the therapy. Only after the client and therapist agree that they are working together to reduce these behaviours and clarify values (see Chapter 23) can they realistically make an agreement or sign a contract to go ahead. Before this work is done, neither party really knows what they are letting themselves in for.

A problem behaviour is a behaviour that is high risk (including all suicidal, self-harming and physically aggressive behaviours), or which stops the person getting help, or which ruins the person's quality of life. It is usually an emotionally driven behaviour and feels out of the client's control.

Part of the task faced by the therapist is to translate the problems the client brings into problem behaviours, which are defined as operationally as possible so that we can see the behaviour in our mind's eye and hope to measure it. For example, Ruth has problem behaviours of self-harm and suicide attempts, but she came to therapy focused on being unemployed, lonely and sad about being bullied as a child. In our interactions, whilst validating her pain, we are working to identify her responses to these circumstances, which we can target for change. This could look something like:

Therapist: So how can I help today?

Ruth: Well I'm just so miserable and lonely all the time I just don't feel life is worth living.

Therapist: I'm very sad to hear that. That must make your life hard. Have you tried to change things at all?

Ruth: Oh, lots of times. I make friends but they always let me down.

Therapist: Yes, people can be horrible. But not everyone is like that – have you never had good times with people?

Ruth: Yes, but it always goes wrong.

Therapist: Well, we can work with you if you're willing – but not with the rest of the human race! Would you be willing to spend some time looking to see if you do anything to contribute to things going wrong?

Ruth: Like what?

Therapist: Like choosing the kinds of people that let you down, or behaving in ways that push people away.

Ruth: Oh yes! I do that a lot.

Therapist: Push people away? OK, I can see why you might do that if you're scared of being let down. Maybe we can talk more about what you do that ends up pushing people away?

Mindfulness and validation

As mindfulness is at the centre of CBT+, these discussions of problem behaviours should be held from a standpoint of compassionate mind. Spotting judgements in our own responses and in the client's story about their own behaviour is helpful in raising awareness. Using our knowledge that judgements will be taking place, we can make efforts to notice when they are happening. The therapist can then reframe their own judgements. The therapist can also begin to educate the client to notice his/her own judgements and model how to speak non-judgementally wherever possible, using a mindful 'observe and describe' approach. Here is an example:

Ruth:	I'm so stupid I can't spot a person who's likely to let me down.
Therapist:	Could we rephrase that without the judgement words? How about 'I don't have the skills yet to select the people who are likely to be good for me?'
Ruth:	Hmm … ok … do you think I could learn how to do that, then?

Shame-busting

As well as identifying and operationalising problem behaviours, we are building a therapeutic alliance with the client. Developing trust and openness takes time and effort on both parts. However, holding the problems lightly, as in ACT, whilst validating the person's pain, as in DBT, allows us to begin 'shame busting' early. One way to do this is to present the client with a set of six problem clouds (see Figures 21.1–21.6). These are downloadable from www.getyourlifeback.global. Therapists who have used these clouds report that clients can simply circle the problems they identify and then pass the paper back across the table, without having to immediately say the problems out loud or discuss each one in detail. Seeing the behaviours laid out in such a matter of fact way serves to normalise the problems and convince clients they are not alone in their struggles. Here are the six clouds:

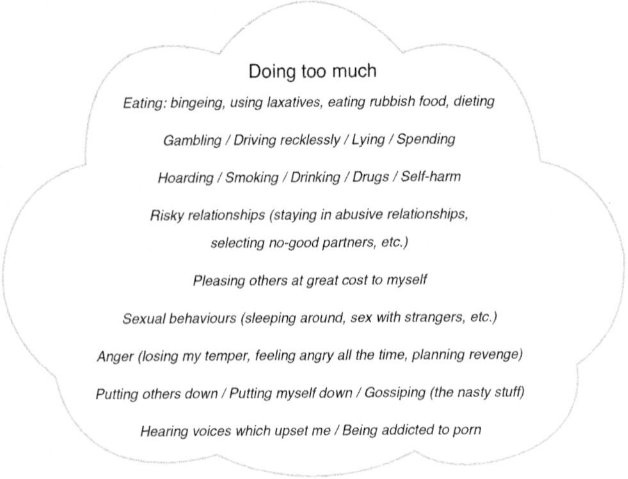

Doing too much

Eating: bingeing, using laxatives, eating rubbish food, dieting

Gambling / Driving recklessly / Lying / Spending

Hoarding / Smoking / Drinking / Drugs / Self-harm

Risky relationships (staying in abusive relationships, selecting no-good partners, etc.)

Pleasing others at great cost to myself

Sexual behaviours (sleeping around, sex with strangers, etc.)

Anger (losing my temper, feeling angry all the time, planning revenge)

Putting others down / Putting myself down / Gossiping (the nasty stuff)

Hearing voices which upset me / Being addicted to porn

Figure 21.1 Problem clouds

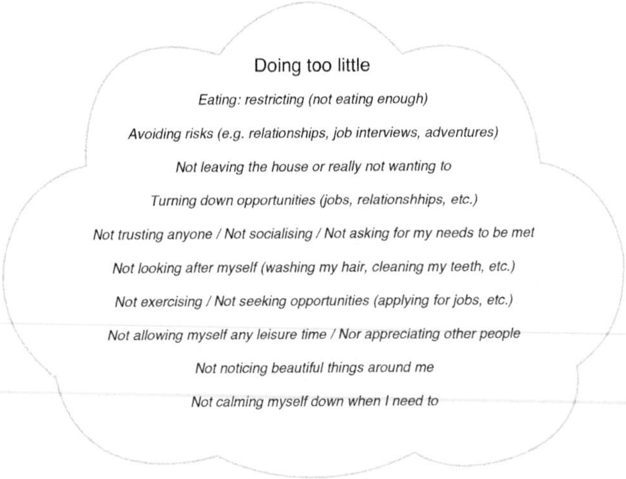

Doing too little

Eating: restricting (not eating enough)

Avoiding risks (e.g. relationships, job interviews, adventures)

Not leaving the house or really not wanting to

Turning down opportunities (jobs, relationshhips, etc.)

Not trusting anyone / Not socialising / Not asking for my needs to be met

Not looking after myself (washing my hair, cleaning my teeth, etc.)

Not exercising / Not seeking opportunities (applying for jobs, etc.)

Not allowing myself any leisure time / Nor appreciating other people

Not noticing beautiful things around me

Not calming myself down when I need to

Figure 21.2

Anxiety

Obsessive Compulsive Disorder (OCD): checking (plugs, locks, etc.)
Compulsive behaviours (hand-washing, hair-pulling, etc.)
Rituals (Counting, doing things in a rigid order, etc.)
Compulsive thoughts, 'What if?' thoughts, angry thoughts, etc.
Illness behaviours (thinking I'm sick, keep on seeing the doctor, etc.)
Worrying (about disasters, about being ill, about being mad, about money, etc.)
Panicking, having panic attacks
Being paranoid (thinking others are out to get me)
Clinging to people
Fearing abandonment, that a loved one might leave me
Predicting disaster
Being afraid of everyday things (going out, being close to others, etc.)
Making plans to deal with every 'What if?' thought
High levels of anxiety after trauma

Figure 21.3

Hopelessness

Hopeless thoughts such as 'It will never work',
'I can't do it', 'what's the point?'
Self-loathing (I am worthless, no good, a failure, stupid, etc.)
Rumination (dwelling on the past – if only, I should have...)
Believing I do not deserve things
Can't see a way forward
Envy (I wish I were my rich neighbour, etc.)
Bitterness (life has treated me badly)
Feeling depressed
Jealousy (I don't trust my partner)
Staying in bed all day
Zoning out

Figure 21.4

Law breaking

Shoplifting

Stalking

Porn (illegal stuff)

Criminal damage

Stealing

Being in a gang and doing law-breaking stuff

Fighting

Physically abusing my partner

Thinking about or planning to harm other people

Harming other people

Cyber-bullying

Trolling

Figure 21.5

Trauma (after bad things happen)

Fashbacks (reliving parts or all of horrible events)

Images and sensations from the trauma/Nightmares

Numbing out (not feeling anything)

Feeling unreal (body unreal or world feels unreal)

Being as if in a fog ('depersonalisation')

Thinking I'll never feel safe again

Staying over-alert for danger

Bad thoughts of blaming myself or others

Irritability / Mood swings

Being jumpy and startling easily

Problems remembering parts or all of the trauma

Concentration problems

Avoiding trauma-related things (the place, people, thoughts, talking about trauma)

Figure 21.6

For example, Stuart came to therapy reporting flashbacks and distress, but did not immediately mention his drinking. He avoided disclosing this, as he was ashamed of it. But he was able to circle 'drinking too much' in the problem cloud, and the therapist was able to quietly note this as part of his target behaviour list and gently enquire more as they got to know each other.

Target behaviour list

A target behaviour list is considered essential in DBT, as it provides the main content of each individual therapeutic session, where the therapist and client work to reduce these behaviours. DBT would also teach new skills to replace the target behaviours in a group setting. In CBT+ the therapist can teach new skills in individual or in group settings. If in individual settings, new skills are often part of values clarification, goal setting and moving towards a meaningful and purposeful life.

The target behaviours should be as clear as possible and defined as operations in the behavioural sense of the word. The therapist should be able to 'see' the behaviours in her mind's eye. For example, here are some of Ruth's target behaviours:

- Overdosing with a mixture of prescription medication ('painkillers') and alcohol
- Cutting my arms with razor blades
- Drinking about a bottle of vodka a day
- Blanking out and not remembering what happened
- Getting distressed about the voices I hear
- Believing that I'm smelly, dirty and worthless
- Getting admitted to the mental health ward regularly

And here are some of Stuart's:

- Getting distressed about the flashbacks I have
- Not having a job

- Drinking excessive alcohol at lunch time instead of eating
- Feeling distanced from my family
- Having panic attacks when driving

As you can see, it is often exposing and difficult for a client to make and face up to such a list. It is helpful to balance this with a list of the client's strengths and resources.

Summary

Naming the problem is more complex than it sounds. The aim of the work is to jointly identify the target behaviours to reduce in the therapy, along with the client's existing strengths and resources. Another aim is to set the expectations for therapy, build commitment on both sides and lay the foundations for a strong working relationship.

22

Build awareness

NAVIGATES

Still working around developing the list of target behaviours, this chapter looks at formulating each one using a more CBT informed approach. Here we are building a non-judgemental awareness of the clients' experience of their own behavior, modelling validation and empathy, and reducing shame and avoidance as we go.

Formulate each behaviour with the client

CBT+ uses the CBT five areas approach (Williams, 2001; Wright, Williams & Garland, 2002). In CBT+ if need be the therapist *guesses* the client's thoughts, feelings, body sensations and behaviours/urges, using the 'Wheel of Experience' as a guide. We do not presume the client has the skills to do this themselves. In this way, the therapist can build a shared awareness both of the client's experience whilst engaging in the behaviours and also her metacognitions or thoughts and beliefs about the behaviours. At the same time, the *contexts* in which each behaviour occurs can be identified, as we explore what typically triggers the behaviours and the setting conditions for the behaviours. This will eventually enable us to explore triggers, and from there the drivers for or functions of each behaviour (see Chapter 24).

Building awareness of thoughts, feelings, body sensations and behaviours during the target behaviours

CBT+, like DBT, does not assume that a client is able to observe and describe the five elements that make up the Wheel of Experience (including the trigger). Validation in DBT can involve *guessing* the thoughts, feelings, behaviours/urges and body sensations a person had or is having, while at the same time checking in with the client to see whether these guesses seem right to them. The question 'How did you feel?' is replaced with something like 'I wonder, did you feel afraid at that point?' At the same time as building awareness, we are educating the client about their own internal events and how to observe and describe them. We are also modelling validation and self-compassion, moving towards developing compassionate mind, as in CFT. By standing together with the client and observing the Wheel of Experience, we are helping the client to defuse (ACT) from these internal events and to increase perspective-taking (CBT). For example, Figure 22.1 shows Ruth's Wheel of Experience just before cutting her arm with a razor blade.

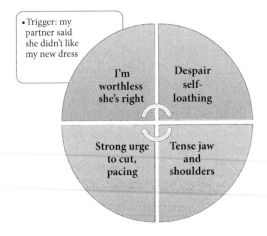

Figure 22.1 Ruth's Wheel of Experience just before cutting her arm

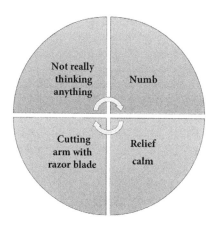

Figure 22.2 Ruth's Wheel of Experience during/immediately after cutting her arm

Figure 22.2 shows her Wheel of Experience during/immediately after cutting.

Building awareness of thoughts, feelings, body sensations and behaviours about the target behaviours

As well as formulating the client's internal experiences *during* the target behaviours, it is important to observe and describe their thoughts, feelings, body sensations and behaviours/urges *about* the behaviours, or their metacognitions. We may find severe self-criticism or helplessness, beliefs about the impossibility of change, frustration and avoidance.

For example:

Ruth: I need to keep my razor blade because cutting is my safety net, it's something I know I can always do if I need to.

Therapist: So, it's your safety net and you think you can't manage without it?

Ruth: Yes, that's right.

Stuart: I've tried to stop drinking … every morning I say I'm not going to do it, but every lunchtime I find a reason why I should just do it for one more day … or I don't think at all and just do it.

Therapist: That must be very frustrating for you when you're thinking about it now. Does it make you feel helpless, like there's no point trying?

Stuart: Yes, there are periods when I just resign myself to how it is. And I think I must be a weak person who can't control his urges.

Building awareness of how the target behaviours keep life restricted and distressing and the need to stop doing them

At this point the therapist needs to get commitment from the client to work on reducing the target behaviours. One way to do this is to use the pros and cons commitment strategy. The client is asked to list both the pros and cons of the target behaviour. This allows consideration of the ways in which a behaviour is working both for a person as well as the advantages of stopping doing it.

Stuart's pros and cons for stopping drinking at lunchtime are shown in Table 22.1.

Therapist: I need you to know the therapy's going to involve us committing to you stopping the drinking at lunch times … we can see from the pros and cons list it's interfering with your health, family relationships, finances and self-respect; it'll be almost impossible for us to make progress whilst all these aspects of your life are being damaged in this way.

Stuart. I know what you're saying. I just get this feeling of frustration and despair when I think about trying and failing yet again. I don't want to let my family, or you, down.

Table 22.1 Stuart's pros and cons

Pros	Cons
I'll be healthier	I might fail again
I'll have more self-respect	I'll have horrible feelings I can't get rid of without using the drink
Be able to be around my family without being conscious of my breath	I may not be able to manage
Not being under the influence, so really being myself	I might not like my real self
More cash available for other things	I might end up worse than when I started
Satisfaction of success	
Feeling like a normal dad	

Therapist: I can understand your fears, especially as you've tried before. And the choice has to be yours. If you're willing to give it a go, I can help with new skills to handle the horrible feelings – and you'll have me alongside you this time. On the other hand, I can see it's a big commitment and of course I would respect your decision if you choose to carry on drinking. It's just, you don't need me to help with that!

Summary

The process of building awareness, in this case of problem behaviours, continues throughout therapy. At this early stage it allows preliminary formulation, validation and building commitment to change. In parallel, a collaborative relationship of mutual respect is being developed.

References

Williams, C. J. (2001). *Overcoming Depression: A Five Areas Approach.* London: Arnold.

Wright, B., Williams, C., & Garland, A. (2002). Using the Five Areas cognitive–behavioural therapy model with psychiatric patients. *Advances in Psychiatric Treatment, 8*(4), 307–315.

23

Clarify values

NAVIGATES

In this chapter we are going to show how to identify the client's values. The reason for this is that CBT+ focuses on helping the client to thrive, by building a meaningful and purposeful life, not just on reducing symptoms. Values will also be central to maintaining motivation and persistence in the face of setbacks.

Both ACT and DBT place emphasis on identifying goals and values as a main part of therapy and as a key indicator when thinking about outcome. Although it seems obvious and easy to clarify values at first sight, one soon discovers that it can be subtle and difficult. Somehow, it is hard to pin down where to start and what processes to engage in to achieve values clarification. In addition, many clients have learned through bitter experience to avoid setting goals or being clear about their values because of a history of perceived failure.

Introducing values to clients

There are different methods of clarifying values. The ones shown here are mostly drawn from ACT and from DBT. CFT contains a strong explicit value of having compassion and empathy towards self and others. In CBT+ we bring an awareness of the essential nature of compassion to our work. When introducing values, the therapist can speak about the nature of suffering – the Buddhist perspective is that suffering comes from futile efforts to avoid pain.

ACT teaches that we can bring meaning and purpose to our lives by developing acceptance, or willingness to experience unpleasant emotions, in the interest of focusing on our values and achieving values-related goals. If we take 'committed action' to follow our values, we can reduce suffering and become willing to accept inevitable pain. On a simpler level, as in DBT, the therapist can introduce values work as a way of identifying the reasons for doing therapy. This allows us to evaluate therapy outcome by asking whether the client is living a life consistent with their values (rather than whether they feel better or have fewer symptoms). It means that at times of low motivation, the therapist and client can both step back and recommit to the whole purpose of the exercise, refocusing on values, taking a longer-term perspective.

Methods of clarifying values

It is helpful to identify important areas of the client's life. The basic four areas are relationships, health, work (or 'occupation' or 'how I spend my day') and leisure/personal growth. Other areas may include spiritual life, contribution to society, respecting other species, conserving the planet. Some cultures prioritise one's role in the family and/or society, or doing one's duty. Here are a few sentence-completion examples. Note that we direct the focus to *what sort of person* the client would like to be.

> In my relationships I would like to be …
> In my health I would like to be …
> In my job/how I spend my time I would like to be …
> In my leisure/personal growth I would like to be …

The client may respond with, for example, trustworthy, loving, assertive and other adjectives that describe how they would like to be in their relationships, and likewise for the other areas.

Each of the areas identified can be broken down further. For example, the relationships area could be broken down into relationship with our spouse or significant other, relationships with children, relationships with colleagues, relationships with friends and relationship with self. As mentioned previously, some clients may have real difficulty in articulating values. This may be because of avoidance (conscious or unconscious), or it may be because this exercise feels very new and unfamiliar. The therapist may have to provide many examples or share some of their own values to prompt the client.

Other tools for clarifying values include values cards. Each card contains an adjective and the client sorts the cards in order of importance. A useful metaphor from ACT involves imagining one's eightieth birthday party where we are allowed to invite anyone we have ever loved respected and admired (whether they are actually alive or dead today), and each of these people will make a speech about us. Our task is to identify what we would want to hear them say about us. When people do this exercise, they usually find they focus on being loved, being a kind person, etc., rather than fabulously clever or successful.

One more route to values clarification involves using a 'values bull's-eye', a technique originally developed by Tobias Lundgren. Here, we first generate values statements using one of the techniques above, or in any other way. Then we use a dartboard or archery board diagram (see Figure 23.1). This is divided into four or more values areas. The task is to step back and assess overall how you are currently living your life compared to your ideals as described in your values statements, putting a cross on the board near to the bull's eye if you feel you are living according to your values, further out if not.

Troubleshooting values work

Values can only be about ourselves, not about other people: a common difficulty is that the client comes up with value statements such as 'In my relationships, I want to be loved'. Of course, we are unable to determine the behaviour of those around us. Similarly,

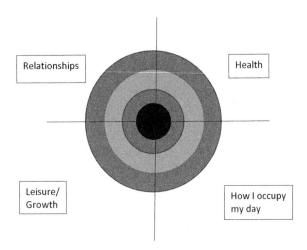

Figure 23.1 Value bull's-eye

'being successful' often depends as much on our context as on ourselves. But we can state that we value behaving in loving ways towards other people, that we would value being able to accept the love of another person, etc. The therapist may have to help the client rephrase their value statements in ways that lie within their own capability.

Impossible values

Sometimes clients state that they want to be perfect, or never make mistakes, or be stricter with themselves. These statements can reflect the psychological inflexibility and perfectionism that is maintaining their distress. At this point the therapist may need to intervene to reframe the values in more compassionate language. Suggesting adding a value of being 'kind in my relationship with myself' can be useful here. Some clients may value being better than everyone else in one way or another: a reframe is called for.

Clashing values

When we start to work towards our values by translating them into goals and then taking baby steps towards them (see later chapters), we may find values clash. For example, being a reliable work colleague and a supportive available father may not always go together. This means that prioritising certain values and understanding that priorities may change is important here.

In general, however, the guiding principle is that clients choose their own values and the therapist respects their choice, so long as they are workable in practice.

Client examples

Ruth

Ruth struggled to clarify values as she believed she was worthless. With encouragement from her therapist she did say that she valued being a kind person in her relationships. She was very tuned in to other people's needs. The therapist managed to negotiate adding a value of kindness to herself. This helped Ruth see that if other people deserved her kindness, she too could receive some from herself. Her 'bull's eye' relationships area had to be divided into two sub-areas, one for relationships with others, where she was living close to her values, and one for relationship with self, where she was living far away from her values. Later in the therapy Ruth went back and added 'being assertive' to her relationships with others value area.

Stuart

Stuart was very clear about his values, but clarifying them brought him face to face with the fact that he was no longer living them. Since the accident he felt like a different person and unable to live according to his values: to be a loving father and husband and reliable provider for his family. This caused a lot of shame and reluctance to discuss his values. The therapist did a lot of hope-giving and 'cheerleading', reassuring Stuart that it was a realistic goal to get into a new place where he could once again live closer to these values. She informed him of the effectiveness of trauma-focused interventions and described the recovery of other clients. She also stressed that such recovery required revisiting the trauma in great detail, which might be painful as well as healing. In this context, the therapist was using values work to increase willingness and commitment to engage in therapy.

24

Investigate the behaviour

NAVIGATES

This chapter shows how to analyse the function of a behaviour and then how to change it. We start by returning to a central focus of contextual behavioural therapy, functional analysis. The aim in CBT+ is to come to a shared understanding with the client of why the problem behaviours keep recurring based on behaviour analytic theory, rather than the client's or therapist's intuition or story about the problem.

How to get started

Since we are analysing behaviour, we need to return to the list of problem behaviours prepared with the client during the earlier work. In general, high-risk and high-cost behaviours should be targeted first, in order to make the client's life safer and generate hope for change. For example, we might choose 'Overdosing with pain-killers and alcohol' from Ruth's problem list.

When analysing behaviour, it is important to choose a specific and recent example of the selected behaviour. The therapist can use diary recording of behaviour (a diary is downloadable from www.getyourlifeback.global), or simply ask the client whether the behaviours targeted have occurred this week. Ruth reported overdosing on Wednesday with pain-killers and vodka, so the therapist and client will need to analyse this behaviour. This technique is drawn directly from DBT, with the addition of the CBT Wheel of Experience.

The Wheel of Experience

A useful place to start is with the Wheel of Experience, and it is often easiest to do one wheel for *before* the behaviour and one wheel for *after*. Ruth said she had received a call from her partner, saying she wanted to end their relationship. Here are Ruth's Wheels of Experience: Figure 24.1 before vodka and pain-killers and Figure 24.2 during and just after drinking a bottle of vodka and taking pain-killers.

It can be seen from the contrast between the two wheels, that one function of overdosing is to remove the unbearable emotional pain of rejection. In other words, a negative reinforcement contingency is in place. Negative reinforcement strengthens behaviour by allowing avoidance of, or escape from, aversive (negative) stimuli, in this case the horrible feelings or aversive internal state. The other possibility to look for is positive reinforcement, which strengthens behaviour by producing pleasant internal states.

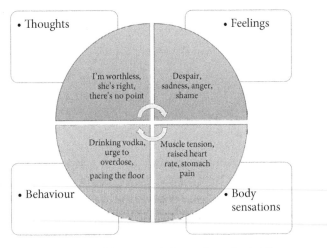

Figure 24.1 Ruth's Wheel of Experience before vodka and pain-killers

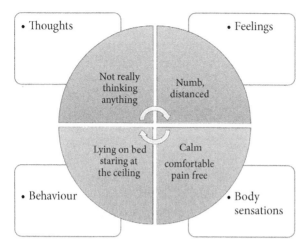

Figure 24.2 Ruth's Wheel of Experience during/just after vodka and pain-killers

Chain analysis

The next step in CBT+ is to weave the elements of the Wheels of Experience into a chain (chain analysis is the DBT term), as shown in Figure 24.3.

Note that in the chain, each link represents thoughts, feelings, behaviour and body sensations. The trigger event is the flash shape; other events can also be added into the chain if needed. The chain continues past the 'short-term gain' and onto the 'long-term pain', the lasting consequences of the behaviour. The aim is for the client to build awareness of the beginning and end of the sequence, as well as of the function of the behaviour (the short-term gain). The long-term pain describes the cost of the behaviour to the client. In Ruth's case hospital admission makes her job situation worse and her feelings of worthlessness are confirmed and strengthened.

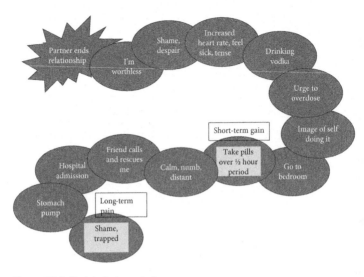

Figure 24.3 Ruth's chain analysis

The vulnerability cloud

Further work is done in CBT+ using the 'vulnerability cloud'. This describes elements of the client's context and life, which causes vulnerability to negative emotional states and impulsive behaviours, moving away from valued actions and goals. Figure 24.4 shows Ruth's vulnerability cloud.

Not having a job means Ruth has a lot of time to ruminate about the past and little cash to spend on things that give her pleasure. It also feeds into her worthlessness belief, which underpins her depressed mood and some of the difficulties in her relationships. Stockpiling meds means she has lethal means available to her most of the time. Constantly drinking vodka means she is more vulnerable to intense overwhelming emotions and impulsive behaviours.

Not having a job
Choosing rejecting partners
Lack of sleep
Vodka habit
Believing I'm worthless
Fear of abandonment
Stockpiling prescription meds in my
bedroom

Figure 24.4 Ruth's vulnerability cloud

Therapist style when carrying out behaviour analysis

This exercise is carried out in collaboration with the client. In general, the experience of analysing a target behaviour is unpleasant for a client, provoking urges to avoid the task and shame, as well as triggering the aversive emotions that occurred at the time. For therapists, there is often a strong urge to avoid the task too. It takes discipline and courage.

Although we are involved in the beginnings of change management here, the therapist style needs to be very validating and compassionate. Validation, where the therapist guesses the emotions, thoughts, behaviours and body sensations of the client, can be very useful during chain analysis.

Focusing on the nano-details of the changes that happen during and after the behaviour is essential, as we need to establish the short-term gain. Yet, when discussing the longer-term costs of the behaviour, we can summarise more, as we simply want to build awareness of how costly the behaviour is and how vicious circles can be involved.

Investigating breaking the links

The next step in the process is to come up with ideas to break the links in the chain and change the elements in the vulnerability cloud. The more ideas the client can come up with the better. It is useful to start with a brainstorming session, where client and therapist together think of anything and everything the client could do differently next time she has an urge to carry out the behaviour, or faces a typical trigger situation. Humour and respectful light-heartedness are often helpful too.

Once a number of options have been identified, the client is invited to choose just three or four options to build into her 'My Breaking the Links Plan', a written document to take away. In Ruth's case, for example, the My Breaking the Links Plan was to:

1) Take the stockpiled meds to the pharmacy
2) Use STOP and paced breathing (see Chapter 29) when the urge to self-harm is triggered by thoughts of my partner
3) Leave the house and seek out the company of my best friend when the urge is strong
4) Call my therapist if I need help putting this into practice

Ruth's therapist was willing to take coaching calls and was supported by a multi-disciplinary team who could organise admission if the therapist could not secure agreement to keep safe. *It is recommended that therapists do not work with severe self-harm or suicide attempts without such support.*

Ruth's therapist checked that Ruth was committed to putting this plan into action, that she was ok to leave the session, then said goodbye. Ruth left the session with a copy of her chain analysis, a My Breaking the Links Plan and a My Breaking the Links Diary where she recorded her experiences of putting the plan into action. All these forms are downloadable from the website.

Following up

It is essential to start the next session with a review of this homework. For example, Ruth may come back and say she has not got rid of the medication stockpile as this is a difficult task for her. The therapist could spend some time doing commitment work, for example a pros and cons list for getting rid of meds.

Session structure

At this stage of the work, most sessions will run as follows:

- Mindfulness (2 mins)
- Set agenda
- Review Breaking the Links Diary
- Recommit client to action if needed
- Review Target Behaviour Diary
- Chain analyse the target behaviour
- Problem solving
- Mindfulness (2 mins)
- Goodbye

This structure involves a high level of discipline on the part of the therapist, and understanding from the client that this needs to be the focus of most sessions. As the target behaviours reduce, there will be increased opportunities to include additional work on elements of the NAVIGATES guideline.

25

Goal setting

NAVIGATES

This chapter involves taking action to move towards valued goals, or 'committed action' and is derived largely from ACT and from CBT. Firstly, we revisit values, shape them up and break them down into manageable steps. Then we help the client commit to taking these steps in everyday life. There should be a movement away from problems, as in the last chapter, and now towards values. Taking action towards getting your life back is not always easy; obstacles to change can prevent valued action happening. It is important to identify and troubleshoot these obstacles.

What is a goal?

A goal is an outcome, small or large, in the client's life, which is in line with the client's values. Taking action towards a goal is a 'committed action'.

Recognising which actions are in line and which are out of line with values

Invite the client to look again at the four values areas in the bull's eye. Without thinking too long or hard, see if they can grab hold of one or two actions last week that were *in line* with their values and one or two which were *out of line*. A form to help with this is available to download at www.getyourlifeback.global. For example, Stuart wrote his key words for each values area and these are shown in Table 25.1.

Table 25.1 Stuart's values and actions

My values	My actions last week
Relationships Be a loving father and husband Be a provider for my family	*In line* – helped children with homework *Out of line* – put off applying for a job
How I occupy my day Using my professional skills to help look after my family	*In line* – researched jobs on line *Out of line* – put off applying for job
Leisure/growth Enjoy hanging out with mates	*In line* – made plan to contact football mates *Out of line* – didn't go out in the evenings
Health Be a fit person	*In line* – phoned gym for an appointment *Out of line* – cancelled slot, too busy

Whilst doing this exercise it is important to shape using non-judgemental language and help the client manage internal judgements. One insight both client and therapist gained was that Stuart gets stuck at the point of actually implementing his good intentions. A problem many of us share! This is connected to the disabling nature of his PTSD symptoms and loss of confidence. He is gradually building awareness that he has many choice-points.

Taking a baby step towards a value

We can actively plan to take steps towards values each day. A good way to start is to use 'baby steps' by identifying one tiny step or goal, which will move us towards a value. This is especially helpful for perfectionistic clients, who may have unrealistic/ambitious goals, or for those with learned helplessness, as baby steps reframe the effort and outcome required.

Choosing one life area from the bull's eye, we help the client identify goals and practical actions (baby steps) they can carry out immediately, using three stages. Here's an example from Ruth:

1. *State value*
   I want to be a person who cares for my health
2. *Imagine how this would look in reality*
   I want to do things that will promote my own health
3. *Identify action/baby step*
   This afternoon, I'm going to prepare a meal with nourishing ingredients

Making this exercise work with a client can be harder than it looks, as it may elicit responses such as 'What's the point?' etc. We can help the client identify these responses as *internal obstacles to change*. As 'homework', or as between-session assignments, we might suggest taking one baby step each day (the same baby step or different ones). The Baby Steps Diary is where the client can record how this goes and note things that get in the way of taking baby steps (obstacles to change). These could be practical problems (lack of time, money, etc.) or messages from the mind ('What's the point?' or 'I'll fail', etc.). Things that help should also be noted. Table 25.2 is an example from Ruth's diary.

Table 25.2 My Baby Steps Diary

Day	Baby step	Did I do it? Yes/no	Things that got in the way	Things that helped
Monday	*Prepare meal with nourishing ingredients*	*Yes*	*Did not have enough veggies in house. Thought I don't deserve all this*	*Had the recipe all ready to go*

Reviewing baby steps and obstacles to change

It is essential to enquire whether the client has completed the task or not during the next session after setting this homework. If she has not completed the diary, there are two options. Either she has forgotten or she has remembered but something got in the way of completing the action. If the problem is forgetting, therapist and client can work on ways to remember next time (sticky notes, phone alerts, etc.). If the problem is an external obstacle, for example, there was an unexpected interruption, we can work on how to make sure the client stays focused enough to carry on with the task after the interruption. If the problem is an internal obstacle, such as a thought such as 'I'll only get this wrong', we can work on reviewing the thought or on mindfully proceeding with the task in the presence of the thought.

For example, Ruth found it useful to have the prompt of the recipe handy, but had not thought about having the ingredients ready. Working on planning ahead would be helpful for her.

Moving from baby steps to short-term goals

Next, therapist and client can design more ambitious goals that will build on the baby steps and move the client faster towards getting her life back. This progression is shown in Figure 25.1.

Ruth noticed that, while taking the baby step of preparing a nourishing meal, she had a powerful thought that she did not deserve such care. She learned a lot about how it can be difficult to move towards goals and values. This is why focusing on whether the client *wants* to do a certain

Figure 25.1 Moving from baby steps to short-term goals

committed action or *likes* doing it or whether it makes her *happy*, is of little use. It is getting our life back that makes us content and at peace with ourselves in the long run. To get there we need to be able to handle all kinds of thoughts and feelings, some wanted, some unwanted.

We would like to add a note here from a contextualist point of view. This is to acknowledge that therapy is often not the complete answer to change. Some obstacles cannot be overcome by individual efforts, as the person may be living in a toxic interpersonal or social environment that is beyond their power to change. We need to work together for social change and not fall into the trap of attributing responsibility for change solely to the individual.

Getting back to Ruth, the therapist suggested that now she had taken some baby steps, she might next think about some short-term goals. These are bigger steps towards being a person who cares for her health. Most people will be familiar with the acronym SMART (Specific, Measurable, Achievable, Realistic and Time limited), which is a helpful aid to constructing short-term goals.

Ruth's short-term goals:

1. Practise mindfulness each day for two weeks
2. Play my guitar at least three times a week
3. Get some physical exercise at least three times a week

She and the therapist made a list of specific actions she could take towards each short-term goal:

1. Practise mindfulness
   - Get some mindfulness recordings
   - Sit for 10 minutes each morning listening to a recording
   - Read about compassionate mind to help with my 'I don' deserve it' thoughts and feelings
2. Play my guitar
   - Buy some new strings for the guitar
   - Dig out my teach yourself guitar book
   - Spend half an hour after lunch each day compassionately playing my guitar

3. Get some physical exercise
    - Get some running shoes
    - Walk briskly for 10 minutes each day
    - Do some yoga stretches when I get home from my walk

Ruth expressed commitment to doing these actions and left the session feeling slightly anxious but excited. She returned the following week with her diary and was pleased that the therapist thought she had done well, even though she had not reached all of her goals.

26

Acceptance of self

NAVIGATES

Developing acceptance of one's self and of others requires relationships involving mutual trust. The affiliation drive, the need to belong socially, is a primary human drive that is a focus in CFT. When we are affiliated, we are relaxed and feel safe, and *new learning* can happen.

Previous chapters have focused on collaboratively reducing target behaviours and taking steps towards values. This work allows both client and therapist to gain confidence in themselves as a team and generates hope and optimism for change. It lays the foundation of mutual trust within an attached relationship, upon which acceptance of self can be built.

This chapter focuses on building awareness and acceptance of self and others. We will find a dialectic in our work, a balance between fact-checking, challenging the client's assumptions about self and others in a similar way to CBT, and more mindful approaches where we help the client to simply observe judgement thoughts and feelings and turn the mind towards valued action.

DBT, ACT, CBT and CFT approaches to acceptance of self and others

All of the therapies, which CBT+ draws upon, place importance on this topic and it is interesting that all of them really focus on it more as therapy progresses, because the work requires the presence of trust and attachment. DBT might address lack of self-acceptance by including 'having thoughts and feelings of self-loathing' in a target behaviours list drawn up with the client. Behaviours that result from and involve self-loathing would also be targeted. These could be self-harm, neglecting self-care, etc. CBT might use a schema-based formulation, identifying core beliefs such as 'I am worthless/defective; others are dangerous' leading to underlying assumptions such as 'Others will discover how worthless I am if they get close to me' and 'I must not trust another person'. These underlie negative automatic thoughts (NATs) such as 'he's trying to trick me'. Core beliefs can be worked on using Socratic questioning, behavioural experiments and chair work. ACT aims for the client to develop a sense of self that transcends internal events such as thoughts and feelings, described as 'self as context', essential for psychological flexibility. Metaphors, defusion and mindfulness all help to gain perspective in ACT. Compassion-focused therapy is particularly strong on self-acceptance, compassion for self and others being the major focus of therapy, using mindfulness and compassionate mind training to develop self-acceptance.

The function of self/other loathing

As always, contextual behaviour therapy practice means we should consider the function of self-loathing before trying to change it. Consider the chain analysis of Ruth's interaction with her partner (see Chapter 24). Ruth directs her anger towards herself. This allows a progression towards self-harm with its distracting and relieving functions, but also protects her hope that her partner is a good and caring partner. Self-acceptance work aims towards clients achieving a 'felt sense' of being acceptable and good enough in their own eyes. One consequence of achieving this is that the client may have to reappraise the actions of significant others, in their past and present lives. For example, Ruth may realise that her partner has always had difficulty making commitments and is likely to leave her again even if they do get back together. She may also realise that her mother was not a 'good-enough' mother and may never be. Some clients are very unwilling to do self-acceptance work, as it can blow all of the protection offered by self-loathing out of the water. If this is the case, it is important to return to commitment and values work, as well as being flexible enough to accept that perhaps, right now, it is impossible for them to proceed with self-acceptance work.

Specific techniques to develop self-acceptance

The four therapies offer a number of techniques to address self and other acceptance, a selection is listed below. It should be remembered that this is a very big step for clients, requiring ongoing work and often needs weaving into other therapeutic work. It will require patience, sensitivity and careful timing from the therapist. Changes achieved will initially be vulnerable to setbacks triggered by various life crises.

Schema formulation

Stuart had a 'good-enough' childhood, but now has a post-trauma presentation. A new set of schemas, about the danger of driving and about his own perceived inadequacy, have been superimposed on pre-existing adaptive schemas, and so we need to formulate both. His good-enough childhood gave him strong values about providing for and protecting his loved ones, but these values now seem impossible to fulfil. His post-traumatic reactions of fight and flight stop him from functioning normally, and his attribution of meaning to these reactions has been that they mean he is weak and unmanly, making him depressed. Sharing this formulation with Stuart allowed him to see things from a new perspective, it was validating and communicated 'It's not your fault' and 'It can change'.

Two chair work

Two chair work is prominent in many therapies and there are many ways to do it. One way is to label the person's negative self-talk and self-criticism as 'the Bully'. The therapist gets the client to become the Bully, sitting in the Bully's chair, saying out loud all the horrible things she thinks to herself every day, directing this towards an empty chair where the client herself is sitting (in imagination). Then she swaps chairs and reflects on how it feels to be spoken to in this way, whether it is helpful, etc. We can then work in various ways. For example, we can encourage her to argue back with the Bully, presenting all the reasons and evidence she is not in fact like this. We might ask her to thank the Bully for all its efforts to prevent her making mistakes, and reassure it that she can take care of herself now.

Passengers on the bus

ACT techniques include metaphors for not engaging with the Bully, such as 'passengers on the bus'. The idea here is that our thoughts and feelings are internal events that distract us from committed action and tell us negative stories about ourselves. Defusing from strongly held beliefs about the self and others is a vital move in self-acceptance. Mindfulness skills mean we can allow the 'passengers' to rage away and criticise whilst we refocus the mind on our current task or activity, of driving our bus towards a more meaningful life.

Perfect nurturer

We first learned this technique from Deborah Lee in a CFT workshop. The therapist invites the client to create an image of a person, spirit, animal, tree, light, etc., to be their 'perfect nurturer'. When people find it difficult to make images they can describe the image in words. Whenever the client is in need of some compassion, wise words or a hug, the client can go to their perfect nurturer in imagination to receive compassion. The therapist can refer to the perfect nurturer throughout the therapeutic work as a useful ally: 'What would your perfect nurturer say?'

Compassionate mind training

Compassionate mind training is central to CFT, which has a range of techniques to increase the client's capacity for and willingness to experience compassion. An example is *the compassionate self*. This involves the client imagining she is a deeply compassionate person, with each of the qualities of compassion – wisdom, strength, warmth and responsibility. The exercise invites the client to fully focus on how it feels to be wise, strong, kind and non-judgemental, including changing the body posture and breath to match these imagined feelings.

Self-as-context

ACT uses metaphors such as striving to be the stage, not the actors upon it; being the chessboard, not the pieces or the players. The aim is to develop the 'observing self' as distinct from the 'thinking self'; that is, a self that is transcendently separate from the internal events that occur in the mind. Achieving this develops resilience in the face of setbacks and negative thoughts and feelings.

Kind hand

The kind hand exercise is found in many therapies and is very useful for prompting an immediate 'drop into' kindness towards self and others. The client is invited to place a hand over her heart and give herself some kindness, allowing herself to feel loved, safe and precious.

Putting yourself in the other's shoes

This exercise is good for empathy with another person. The client is invited to think of a person she knows who irritates the hell out of her. Then to imagine herself saying something the other person typically says. She is asked to imagine truly meaning those words, then to think about the person's history and the reasons why they may sincerely hold these beliefs. Finally, she is asked to try to see things from their viewpoint.

Inner child

This is a well-known metaphor and is so rich in its uses. The client is asked to imagine herself as a little child. The therapist might say:

> Be specific, what age are you, where are you? Who are you with? Now bring your adult self into the equation. What does your inner child need right now? Maybe it is protection, needing to play or a hug. Check out what your child needs a few times a day and give yourself permission to meet those needs.

This exercise can be combined with self-care homework, when the client is asked to take time each day to meet some of the needs identified in this way.

Ruth had very big struggles with all of the work we have described above, finding herself very reluctant to engage with it and moving between periods when she 'felt acceptable' and others when she did not. She had to work alongside a strong sense that she did not deserve any kindness at all.

Summary

Self-acceptance is a major step for many clients to take along their journey. Working to help them, therapists must establish a safe attachment relationship and model acceptance themselves. There are many specific exercises and activities that foster self-accep-tance, yet these cannot be randomly applied without attention to the functions of self-loathing. The client may experience loss (of hope that the other person is kind/available, etc.) when she realises that relationship issues may not have been her fault. And yet, she will gain contentment, resilience and so much more.

27

Tackling trauma

NAVIGATES

This chapter covers the CBT+ approach to trauma, especially exposure approaches. Research has established that re-living and re-scripting are both successful CBT techniques for working with trauma. It is essential to assess whether the trauma is Type 1/Simple PTSD (single or few incidents) or Type 2/Complex PTSD (many incidents, often occurring during childhood development, perhaps involving carers). To undertake Type 2 work, we will be required to pay attention to a more complex set of issues. These include attachment, emotion and impulse regulation, sense of self and sense of meaning, and much longer therapy duration than for Type 1.

The most up-to-date research and clinical expertise suggest that re-living and re-scripting are equally effective. There is an ongoing debate about which clients may or may not benefit from these techniques. It has been received clinical wisdom that people with psychosis and those who lack social support, for example, may be destabilised by these approaches, but there is little research on this. Alternatively, researchers such as Turner et al. (2014) argue that most people can benefit, including those with psychosis. Although it is not covered in this chapter, some therapists also use EMDR (Eye Movement Desensitisation and Reprocessing) – an approach with demonstrated efficacy but poorly understood mechanisms of change.

Some trauma-affected clients cannot remember whether or not they were traumatised. They may deny it despite evidence, or know they were traumatised but have no memory of it. Others have complete blanks where their child memories ought to be. These clients are affected by dissociation, a set of shutting-down responses to trauma, and will need specific interventions before exposure work can take place (see Chapter 15).

Even when clients do have memories of abuse, neglect and trauma, it is important to give psychoeducation about the reconstructive nature of memory. Each time we remember something, the hippocampus collects information from many areas of the brain and constructs imagery (sights, sounds, smells, etc.) along with meanings and emotions. Memory is not a video that can be replayed. Memories are incomplete, biased and can become distorted. These facts need to be communicated, without invalidating the client's own experience and distress. Some clients are unable or unwilling to revisit trauma. In this case low-impact strategies for handling anxiety such as self-soothing, distraction and adaptive avoidance should be used.

Re-living techniques

Re-living techniques involve a re-living (the trauma) session or sessions, followed by debriefing. Further work is done on cognitive restructuring and reducing avoidance behaviour in the real world. This is the trauma-focused approach of Ehlers et al. (2004). Edna Foa's (Foa & Rothbaum, 1998) re-living approach is also popular: this involves the client listening repeatedly to a tape of the re-living until distress levels decrease. In ACT, 'sitting with' or mindfulness exposure approaches to trauma are often used, allowing the client to learn that staying in observer mind and willingly allowing the experience to occur changes the client's relationship with the material. In ACT as in all behavioural approaches, exposure should be interoceptive, imaginal and in vivo to ensure new learning. This may be done by observing how the body feels when elements of a trauma are brought to mind; by going through the trauma in imagination; by visiting the trauma site. CBT+ blends these approaches together to maximise the therapeutic effect.

Here is a description of a typical trauma focused CBT+ re-living session (this basic structure would also be used for a re-scripting session):

1. Re-living begins by asking the client's *informed consent* to go through the trauma in a quite intense way, in order to help relieve the distress and other effects the trauma is having in their life. One useful metaphor is:

    > Your brain could be compared to an office. You may have stored the information about the trauma in a filing cabinet marked 'here be monsters!' When you try to think about the trauma it is very difficult, yet when you are not thinking about it at all sometimes some monsters get out and bother you with images, thoughts or feelings you don't want. What we are doing in a re-living session is opening the filing cabinet together and looking at the monsters, by going through the whole event. We will use the first person and present tense, so you will say 'I am now …' rather than 'Then this happened …'. This should allow the trauma information to be filed in another cabinet marked 'things in the past' so that it will stay back in the time and place it happened.

    The therapist assures the client that she will have complete *control and choice* during the procedure. A signal is agreed, for example, the client holding her hand up to indicate that she wishes to stop. The therapist might say:

    > It is very important that you have control in this re-living. If you choose to stop, I will absolutely respect that choice. Let's practice the signal [client holds up hand]. However, I will probably ask if we can just stay with it for 30 seconds more. This is because at the point you wish to stop you will probably have reached a really difficult moment. If we can get through that moment we

may well get to the end of the scene. If we can do that, we may not have to repeat the exercise again. If you say 'no' when I ask you to continue for 30 seconds, or if you hold your hand up again, we will definitely stop.

2. The therapist tells the client that they will be asked to rate their distress levels as they go through the scene, one being no distress and ten being intolerable. If necessary, the therapist will teach the client how to calibrate their distress this way.

3. The therapist teaches the client *paced breathing*. This is a breathing pattern of four seconds breathing in, six seconds breathing out. This slow breath should not be too shallow or deep and should involve relaxed shoulders and chest if possible. This is to be used, prompted by the therapist, at times when distress levels are too high (nine or ten).

4. Any client questions are invited.

5. The therapist then asks the client to close their eyes and get into the scene, describing the trauma, in the present tense and using the first person. The scene can be set by asking the client: 'Are you present in the scene now? What can you see? Can you smell anything?' It is helpful if the therapist can see the scene in their own mind's eye. Whilst the client is describing the scene the therapist can deepen the experience by asking questions such as 'Now what is happening?' The Wheel of Experience can now be explored, asking the client to observe and describe: 'What is happening in your body right now?' 'How fearful are you feeling right now?' [looking for ratings one to ten and including other feelings as appropriate] 'What thoughts are around now?' The therapist asks for distress ratings at intervals, prompting the use of paced breathing at high levels of distress. The therapist takes notes during the re-living, especially of levels of distress and 'hot spots' of emotion. The therapist also looks for safety behaviours such as opening the eyes, clenching the fists and escape/distancing behaviours, for example, speaking in the past tense or with very flat affect. These behaviours are acceptable if the distress ratings are high, but with low distress ratings

they mean exposure is being prevented and the client should be asked to drop the behaviours. A desirable level of exposure is seven or eight.

6. At the end of the trauma description the client is invited to open their eyes and come back to the room. The therapist will congratulate the client and allow some recovery time.

The therapist then asks the client what they observed about the experience. Often the client's observations are central to the restructuring of their perceptions about the incident and acceptance of some of the effects. For example, one client who was sexually abused realised that he had tried to run away from the scout hut where the abuse took place, but was caught again by his scout leader. This made a huge difference to him, as he had always believed he had somehow wanted the abuse to happen or been passive in his submission to it. Another client had heard the police say at the accident scene 'He's driven through the red light' and blamed himself for the car accident. Upon re-living the event he realised he had not driven through the light but stopped. It was the other driver who had driven through the light.

There is also an opportunity for the therapist to begin some perspective-taking work. For example,

I noticed you had the horrible thought and feeling that you were dying when they were cutting you out of the car. What a terrible thing to experience. Let's just take a minute together to notice that you are not dead.

This may sound strange, but it may be the first time the client has been able to really notice the reality of being alive since the accident

The whole process of orienting, informed consent, agreeing a signal, teaching the breath and the exposure itself should be done in a single session.

Following this session, there is a debriefing session or sessions These focus on emotional 'hot spots' such as 'I thought I would die' or 'It's my fault', inviting the client to look with a new perspective at these thoughts and feelings. Further sessions may involve imaginal or in vivo exposure to avoided situations, such as going to the place where a rape took place or reading newspaper articles about trauma-related events.

Re-scripting

There is increasing interest in imagery re-scripting approaches to trauma. These involve the same procedure as above, but then followed by another session where the trauma script is changed. CBT+ takes the approach of choosing *either* re-living or re-scripting and does not usually carry out both.

A typical re-scripting session may look like this:

The therapist takes the same steps to prepare the client as above, but this time before proceeding adds:

We're going to work on changing what happens in the trauma scene, which we will visit together. This is useful because, although we both know we are using our imaginations to 'change the script', our brains are very good at rewriting memories and changing details. So you will always know what happened and yet your brain will have another 'script' where it can choose to go when you are reminded of the event. This work will allow you to experience new feelings in the scene, involving being in charge of it and being able to escape from it, which we know did not really happen at the time.

As far as possible, the therapist should allow the client to decide how the story will end. However, it may be important to help. One way to help is to suggest a change in the scene that will give the client agency and choice. For example, 'How would it be if, instead of you being the helpless one in the scene, you grew to twice your height and weight? So now you can do whatever you want to do to deal with the situation'. Clients are often delighted with this image and are often surprisingly compassionate in what they decide to do with their abusers and tormentors, though not always. Their decisions will be influenced by their relationship with the perpetrator. Another rule of thumb for re-scripting is that the client should end up being good and being safe.

Having decided on the script, the therapist proceeds as for re-living but at a crucial point, changes the script. The therapist may visit the imagined scene alongside the client and help to rescue or protect them. The client's adult self or 'Perfect Nurturer' may enter the scene and do the same thing. In situations where there is no perpetrator, for example an earthquake or flood, the client may 'resurrect' someone who died so as to be able to say goodbye as they would have liked to. One woman whose baby had died whilst they were fleeing ethnic cleansing was able to carry out in imagination a proper burial of her child according to her cultural customs. Ruth designed a script with her therapist where, when her father was getting into her bed, she became seven feet tall and three feet wide, pushed him onto the floor, picked him up and told him to stay out of her room or she would call the police next time. She told him he was a bad father and did not deserve to have a daughter. Then she made a magic lock for her door that only she could open.

Top CBT+ tips on working with trauma

- It is *not* necessary to approach all the traumatic material in the client's history unless it is causing current distress
- It is vital to have the client's consent to approach trauma
- The therapist ensures the client is stable and has skills to handle emotional distress before proceeding
- There should be psychoeducation for the client about the constructive nature of memory
- Attention should be paid to the meaning the client brings to the experience and to validating the client's distress

- Re-living and re-scripting templates are an effective way to tackle post-traumatic stress
- After exposure work involving traumatic material there should be a debriefing period for the client to allow them to reassign meaning and notice what they have achieved
- There may need to be a period of 'restabilising' the client, or helping them to adapt to life without extreme emotions
- Some clients are unable or unwilling to revisit trauma. In this case *low impact* strategies for handling anxiety should be used

In conclusion, we have at our disposal very effective strategies for dealing with trauma. It is strongly recommended that therapists attend training and get supervision to practice these skills before going ahead.

Suggested further reading

Stopa, L. (2009). *Imagery and the Threatened Self: Perspectives on Mental Imagery and the Self in Cognitive Therapy*. London: Routledge.

References

Ehlers, A., Clark, D. M., Hackmann, A., McManus, F., & Fennel, M. (2004). Cognitive therapy for post-traumatic stress disorder: Development and evaluation. *Behaviour Research and Therapy, 43*(4), 413–431.

Foa, E. B. & Rothbaum, B. A. (1998). *Treating the Trauma of Rape: Cognitive Behavioral Therapy for PTSD*. New York: Guilford Press.

Turner, D. T., van der Gaag, M., Karyotaki, E., & Cuijpers, P. (2014). Psychological interventions for psychosis: A meta-analysis of comparative outcome studies. *American Journal of Psychiatry, 171*(5), 523–538.

28

Exposure and emotions

NAVIGATES

This chapter covers exposure work as well as the need to assess and develop emotional 'literacy' in clients. We have chosen to cover them together, as the maintaining factors in many problem behaviours involve emotional avoidance and emotional dysregulation. We have seen in Chapter 24 that often the function of a target behaviour is that it allows escape from or avoidance of negative emotions. So much of the exposure work we will do with clients involves exposure to emotions. The previous chapter on trauma work is a special case of this, but there is a much wider application of exposure work too.

Emotions

What is an emotion? Emotions can be defined as involving the whole Wheel of Experience – that is, thoughts, feelings, body sensations and behaviour/urges. Emotions may occur in response to internal or external events/stimuli. As shown in Chapter 11, neglect, abuse and invalidation in childhood have dramatic effects on adult emotions: as children, our clients may not have learnt to identify their own emotions correctly; expression of appropriate emotions may have been punished or ignored; expression of inappropriate emotions may have been reinforced. Clients may have learned to truncate their emotions, shutting down or dissociating in response to them. This prevents natural healing by grieving or being able to express anger and other emotions. Positive emotions may be suppressed, consciously or pre-consciously, as they have become associated with disappointment, humiliation or other negative experiences.

Assessing and teaching about emotions

In order to work with emotions, it is helpful to assess:

1. Whether the client has a language for her emotions, or is unable to describe internal states
2. Whether she is comfortable sharing her emotions or has a history of such sharing being punished

This will help direct our work on emotions. We may need to teach a language of emotions and/or work towards allowing and reinforcing appropriate emotional expression.

Teaching emotions can be done didactically, as in the emotion regulation skills module from DBT. In the book *Get Your Life Back*, we provide a table of emotions, listing the name, purpose and Wheel of Experience for each emotion. We can also watch videos, for example, soap operas, with our clients, pausing the screen at emotional moments to mindfully observe and describe the facial and body language, the responses of others, how a given emotion might feel in the body. Diaries are useful to help the client record and rate the intensity of emotions experienced each day. This work is an essential prerequisite for emotion regulation work, as described in the next chapter.

Exposure

CBT has a strong protocol for graded exposure, using a hierarchy of situations rated by the client as relatively easy to relatively difficult. The client is taught relaxation or paced breathing as an emergency measure in case she becomes too distressed to stay in the present. Then the therapist invites the client to visit the scary situations in real life (in vivo) or in imagination (imaginal). The client is asked to describe what she is thinking, feeling, body sensations and behavioural urges as she stays in the situation. Subjective units of distress (SUDs) or client ratings of distress (one to ten) are used to manage the procedure. Ratings of less than seven usually mean insufficient exposure. In this case we need to watch out for 'safety behaviours', things the client may be doing to prevent exposure, such as refusing to close her eyes, counting, squeezing her hands together, etc. Ratings of ten usually mean the client will not be able/willing to stay in the present and we need to use relaxation or breathing to calm the system down a little whilst staying present in the exposure situation. The received wisdom has always been that we should encourage the client to stay present until a reduction of SUDs to, say, four or less, is achieved. This approach is based on a 'habituation' model, meaning that the exposure work leads to a reduction in intensity of response, the same way as pressing on a nerve eventually leads to habituation and a reduction in firing.

As mentioned previously, recent work suggests that exposure works by allowing new learning to occur. That is, the client makes a distinction between 'then and there' and 'here and now'. The brain learns that there is, in fact, no present danger, only past danger. The therapist can be alongside the client in an accepting way, allowing her to keep the 'here and now' perspective whilst observing the 'then and there' event even when SUDs are not reduced. They remain useful, however, as measures of whether or not exposure is occurring. As an outcome with this approach, we may be looking for increased *willingness* to place oneself in difficult situations that may trigger distress responses, and increased ability to manage such responses.

CFT focuses on transforming emotions, to increase experience of compassion. DBT uses mindfulness to sit with intense emotions and also teaches clients how to 'down regulate' them. CBT transforms emotions by transforming thinking. ACT is more focused on 'sitting with' emotions. In our experience, a lot of exposure work is about exposure to emotions.

In CBT+ the therapist must decide whether to work to change an emotion or to change the client's *relationship* with that emotion.

What might guide our decision? One useful distinction, from DBT, is to ask whether a particular emotion is 'warranted' or 'unwarranted'. For example, Ruth's deep shame about her past abuse is clearly unwarranted. Whatever she did or was made to do, or was done to her as a child, cannot be her responsibility. In this case, it can be very helpful to review her beliefs about the past, using Socratic questioning. We could also use compassion-focused work to increase her kindness towards her inner child. Or we could take a more radical ACT approach of letting go of asking whether the emotion is warranted or unwarranted and just practising allowing it to be there whilst we get on with values-based actions.

Here is an example of exposure to emotions work with Ruth. Together, Ruth and the therapist chose an emotion that is part of her target behaviour chain, shame. They chose a *specific situation* from the latest behaviour chain, when her partner ended the relationship. Ruth gave her consent that the therapist would decide when the exercise should end, though she had a 'stop' signal to use if necessary. With Ruth's consent, the therapist asked her to place herself back in the situation when she had just heard this news. She was invited to experience the shame and the therapist sat with her as Ruth described how that felt in her body, what behaviour urges went with it and what thoughts came to mind. They did this for some time, whilst the therapist guided the mindful observations, also asking Ruth to rate the intensity of the shame, using paced breathing/relaxation when the ratings hit nine or ten. Lots of validation and encouragement was provided. Afterwards, the therapist congratulated Ruth on her courage in being willing to experience that horrible emotion. She was also invited to notice the variations in levels of intensity during the exercise, and also to notice what is was like to have that emotion without acting on the urges that go with it. In further sessions, more cognitive work was done on reviewing whether the shame was warranted, and compassion-focused work on feeling empathy towards herself in that horrible situation.

29

New skills

NAVIGATE**S**

In this chapter we cover a whole range of skills that we all need in order to be more or less in charge of the choices we make. These skills can be taught didactically, in groups, individually or introduced during the course of therapy. For very dysregulated clients, it may be necessary to schedule specific skills-focused sessions, separate from sessions on reducing target behaviours. This is because clients can become so emotionally distressed when talking about problems that we cannot steer the session. In any case, although skills come last in NAVIGATES, they are not necessarily the last thing that happens in therapy. In CBT+ we see assessing and increasing skills as an activity that will happen throughout the work. This chapter covers skills for handling thoughts, feelings, body sensations and behaviours/urges.

Assessing skills

There are two main possibilities:

- The client has a skill but does not use it, especially not in her own life
- The client does not have the skill

In the first case, we need to look at obstacles that prevent the client using her skills. In the second, we need to first teach the skills and then make sure that they are used.

Skills for handling thoughts

We recommend a comprehensive chapter on thought handling in the book *Get Your Life Back: The Most Effective Therapies for a Better You*. Here is a summary of skills for handling thoughts.

Validation

CFT and ACT both emphasise the evolutionary survival function of being biased towards the worst that could happen, and also of constantly comparing oneself to others (it is important not to be bottom of the pack). We can validate not the negative thoughts themselves but the fact that we all have them and that is normal.

The naughty puppies metaphor

We use the metaphor of the mind being like a yard full of naughty 'thought puppies', untrained and causing chaos. Our task is to catch the puppies and train them and not be pulled every which way by them. Collars, leads and a lot of training are needed.

Catching thoughts

A first step in handling thoughts is being able to observe and describe them; a second is to lose our judgements about them; a third is to gain perspective on them. Thought records act as 'thought catchers', which help clients identify thoughts and the feelings associated with them. Discussing thoughts together non-judgementally can move the client towards new perspectives. 'Thought puppies' can be positive, miserable, anxious, angry, shaming, guilty, etc. We can discuss with clients how such thoughts can take us away from the life we want to be living; thoughts themselves are internal obstacles to change.

Ways to use a new perspective

Having achieved some degree of shared perspective on thoughts, we have two options: review and challenge thoughts or leave them be and refocus. Reviewing and challenging thoughts is central to CBT and can be done using Socratic questioning, for example, 'What would someone who disagrees with you say?' and by providing a list of thinking errors such as catastrophising and overgeneralisation. We can test out predictions made by the naughty puppy thoughts by planning behavioural experiments. The 'leave them be' option involves not changing the thoughts but our relationship to the thoughts. This is more consistent with ACT: here we get the thought puppies on leads and take them along with us towards our values. ACT offers metaphors such as passengers on the bus and demons on the boat, where the protagonist learns that internal obstacles like thoughts can only rant and threaten, without causing harm.

Thought soldiers

A nice mindfulness exercise is 'thought soldiers'. We make an image of soldiers (or ants, ladybirds, etc.) marching through our heads from left to right then out of the ear, down the arm, across to the other arm and back into the head. Once our chosen marchers are marching, we begin to give each thought as it arises to a soldier.

Compassionate thinking

Compassionate mind training has many examples of how to think compassionately. Here is a practice from Buddhism (which is altered slightly for our client group). Sitting mindfully, bring to mind a good friend. Send them good wishes, for example, 'May you be calm, know peace, may you be loved, etc.'. Once that is done, send the same wishes to a relative stranger, then to someone you find difficult or dislike, then to yourself.

Getting a perspective: helicoptering and stand back and step up

'Helicoptering' is the process of rising up and hovering above the situation one is in, and looking down on it. Then making a decision how to proceed according to one's long-term goals and values. 'Stand back and step up' is exactly that: take a physical or mental step back from the situation, consider the most effective way to behave, then proceed.

Labelling the mind

'Labelling the mind' is very useful for anxiety and rumination. For example, when a client has thoughts of having a heart attack, cancer, etc., she could learn to label this 'Health Anxiety Mind' (HAM). Then, when thoughts to do with health anxiety come along, she can learn to just label them and leave them be. The therapist can ask, 'How is HAM today?'

Skills for handling feelings

Feelings, like thoughts, are internal events and are often dependent on how we are thinking. We can either change or sit mindfully with feelings.

The intensity of feelings can be reduced by:

Self-soothing: stroke a cat, take a warm bath, hug yourself, etc.
Comparisons: think of a person or people in a worse situation
Improve the moment: give yourself a treat, take a break, do something you love doing
Opposite to emotion expression or action: when feeling angry, half-smile, when sad, full smile, when afraid, do something scary

We can mindfully 'sit with' feelings using:

> Physicalising exercise: bring to mind a painful feeling, locate it in the body. Using your hands take it out of the body and look at it, observe and describe its weight, colour, texture, etc. Put it back in
>
> Anchoring onto the breath: in the face of a painful feeling, drop the anchor of the awareness onto the breath and gently keep it there
>
> Observe and describe (labelling the feeling): 'I notice I am having a very sad feeling ...'

Skills for handling body sensations

To change body sensations one can use exercise, diet, sleep, self-soothing, Tai Chi, yoga, music or dance. For clients with a 'bad touch' history, good touch can be used (if the client is willing): massage, spa, holding hands, cuddling a partner or a pet. Mindfulness to body sensations involves observe and describe: 'I notice I am having a feeling of pain in my hip'. Another mindfulness approach involves focusing the mind elsewhere, rather than on the pain, for example, on the breath, on external stimuli or on the task one is doing, and just allowing the body sensation to be there.

Skills for handling behaviours and urges

- STOP and TIP skills from the 'crisis survival' module of the *DBT Skills Manual*: STOP: Stop, Take a breath/step back, Observe the situation, Proceed with awareness
- TIP: change the Temperature of the face (cold water), Intense exercise (star jumps, running), Paced breathing (four seconds in six seconds out)

- Catching behaviours: using urges as indicators of the 'beginning' of a behaviour, we can record urges and rate their intensity on a scale of zero to five
- 'Urge surfing' involves mindfulness to one's urges: sitting with an urge without acting on it can be a new experience for clients
- 'Defusing': separating the observing self from the behaving self – 'I am not my behaviours'
- Forgiveness: behaviour change requires endless practice and so kindness and forgiveness towards oneself is needed to keep going

Practice

Lastly, it is very important for clients and therapists to realise that practice is needed for change. Sometimes discussing how many years the client has been engaging in the target behaviour is useful for putting things in perspective: 'You have been practising shouting at people for 30 years now ... how long have you been practising the STOP skills so far?'

Suggested further reading

Linehan, M. M. (2014). *DBT Skills Training Manual, Second Edition*. New York: Guilford Press.

30

Summary and conclusions

As we come to the end of this book, we hope you have found it thought-provoking and useful. Please use it alone or in tandem with our self-help book to steady yourself on the journeys of acceptance and change you undertake with your clients. The theories underlying the four therapies we have integrated, whilst presenting some apparent contrasts and contradictions, have sufficient in common for us to take a contextual, behaviourally and cognitively informed approach to designing our integrated therapy. Practically, the integration of the therapies has produced a rich tapestry of perspectives and options for the therapist.

The acronym NAVIGATES has proved helpful to us and been well received by participants in the many courses we have delivered so far on CBT+. It can serve as a guide to ensure a sense of direction and a checklist to ensure all the therapeutic bases are covered. Other clinicians who have tried this approach report it as validating their own practice, which often already involved informal integrations of theory and practice from different therapies.

We are aware that this approach has no unique evidence base and relies on the evidence supporting the therapies we have chosen to integrate. We would be delighted to collaborate with any researchers who wish to investigate the effectiveness of CBT+.

Please feel free to download any resources you need from www. getyourlifeback.global or to communicate directly with us. We will be happy to answer your queries or discuss issues. There are several groups of therapists already meeting to support each other in their practice of CBT+; we may be able to connect you.

In conclusion, we hope you find this book a welcome companion and enjoy using it as much as we have enjoyed creating it.

Index

Page numbers in *italics* refer to figures. Page numbers in **bold** refer to tables.

Printed in Great Britain
by Amazon